Churches on Exmoor

The London Borough of Croydon
Co-ordinating Committee for the
DUKE OF EDINBURGH'S AWARD SCHEME

Churches on Exmoor

Foreword by HRH Prince Edward.

Sharmila S. Prabhu

First published in Great Britain in 1992 by
The London Borough of Croydon Co-ordinating Committee
for the Duke of Edinburgh's Award Scheme
c/o DoE Award Centre
Lanfranc High School
Mitcham Road
Croydon CR9 3AS

British Library Cataloguing in Publication Data
A catalogue record for this book is available from the British Library.
ISBN 0 9519003 0 7 Churches on Exmoor (PbK)
ISBN 0 9519003 1 5 Churches on Exmoor (Cased)

Printed and limp bound in Great Britain by Eyre & Spottiswoode Ltd
London and Margate

Case Bound by Cedric Chivers Ltd, of Bristol
Bookbinders and Paper Conservation Specialists
Typeset by JEC Potters & Son Ltd, Stamford
in association with Type Studio, Peterborough.

CHURCHES ON EXMOOR

I dedicate this book to all those who encouraged and guided me during my DoE days, and to all those who subsequently inspired and helped me to continue my involvement, locally and nationally, with various projects associated with the award scheme including the transformation of my most ordinary DoE Gold Award project work into this book.

Sharmila S. Prabhu

This book has been sponsored by

The Nestlé Company Ltd

Coopers & Lybrand Deloitte

Duke of Edinburgh's Award Scheme

Croydon DoE Commercial
Project Committee

Robert Horne Paper Company Ltd

Olives Paper Limited

CK Litho Ltd

PROMT–CM SERVICES

Printed and limp bound in Great Britain by Eyre & Spottiswoode Ltd.

Case Bound by Cedric Chivers Ltd,
Bookbinders and Paper Conservation Specialists

Typeset by JEC Potters & Son Ltd,

Contents

BUCKINGHAM PALACE

I am delighted to be invited to write a few words of introduction to this book; first and most obviously because it represents a project of such exceptionally high quality. The Expedition Section of The Duke of Edinburgh's Award must, like all other Sections, be undertaken in a participant's leisure time and this book is an outstanding example of the amount of effort that is put into an Award Project. My second reason for pleasure when I read about Sharmila's exploits was that she had chosen to explore Exmoor and write about a specific aspect of it, rather than to undertake an expedition in which the journey would be the most important part.

I wish Sharmila Prabhu every success with this book.

Edward

1990

Speaker's House Westminster London SW1A 0AA

I first met Sharmila Prabhu at the launch of The Volunteers in St. James's Palace on the 25th April 1991, when I was delighted to discover that she was a constituent! She was selected to make a speech on this occasion which impressed us all. Having successfully obtained her Bronze and Silver Duke of Edinburgh's Award, she chose as her topic for the Exploration Section of the Gold Award "Churches on Exmoor".

This book is the result of her exertions, and I warmly commend it. It demonstrates in an admirable way how young people can develop, not only physical fitness (The National Park is extensive!), but the ability to write in a way which arouses the enthusiasm of the reader.

Having read this admirable book, I am anxious to take to the moors in order to see for myself some of the historic and beautiful buildings which Sharmila has so vividly describes. I hope you may feel the same.

The proceeds for the sale of the book will be shared between the Duke of Edinburgh's Award Scheme and the upkeep and preservation of Exmoor's lovely Churches. I warmly commend it to you.

Bernard Weatherill

Speaker.

Objectives For Publication

Extracts from the document "Publication Plan and Financial Proposals" produced by Mr Colin J Renwick, then the Hon. Secretary, Croydon Co-ordinating Committee for the Duke of Edinburgh's Award Scheme, Croydon Commercial Project.

CHURCHES ON EXMOOR

A project by Sharmila S. Prabhu in October 1987

"Throughout 1987 Sharmila S. Prabhu was working towards her Gold Award in the Duke of Edinburgh's Award Scheme ... Her project, which is the subject of this document, was carried out alone rather than in a group which is a norm, and the resulting manuscript has been described as a model of its type and one of excellence ..."

PRODUCT

"A superb work carried out by Sharmila S. Prabhu whilst undergoing the exploration section of the Gold Award of the Duke of Edinburgh's Award Scheme".

SOME OF THE OBJECTIVES FOR PUBLICATION:

"To recognise the superb work carried out by Sharmila and to publish it. In doing so put the work as an example to other young people striving to achieve on the scheme ... To produce a product that is within financial reach of young people ...".

Preface

As explained in the Introduction to the Project, "Churches on Exmoor" arose from the need to write a project for the Exploration Section of the Gold Award.

However, as you can imagine, not all projects are published into books, especially into one with a generous foreward by HRH Prince Edward. It all started back in 1987. After completing the project and receiving an assessment, it came to the attention of the Croydon DoE Committee. They felt that it could be used to demonstrate, not only to existing and potential participants but also to industry and prospective employers, what can be achieved through the Scheme.

The transformation from project to book has taken so long. This has been due mainly to the unfortunate timing of the fund raising, ie in the middle of the economic recession.

As a reader, I would like you to bear in mind that the book has been published from the project which was written by a 19 year old and was not directly intended as a guide book. As the aim of the publication was to demonstrate what a Gold Award project could achieve, I have not edited, altered or amended any of the main text.

However, having said that, I believe that the book can be used as a guide to some of the churches on Exmoor. I emphasise "some" as it only covers those that were covered in the original project.

The benefits of using this book as a guide are that architectural and other terminologies are highlighted in italics and are explained in the Glossary. Also, sketch plans are included to enable the reader to appreciate the layout of the church at a glance and to see where some of the main structures of interest are located in the church.

When researching the project, I used a number of sources: first-hand observations, discussions with local people, leaflets available in the churches and some books. However, I could not find any one book that covered all, or the majority, of these churches. Therefore, this book should fill the existing gap.

I hope that you will find "Churches on Exmoor" enjoyable, interesting and informative and that as a result, you will be more aware of the achievements of the Duke of Edinburgh Award Scheme participants and the opportunities that the Scheme offers to young people.

All proceeds from this book (after printing costs) will go to either the church in which it has been sold or to the DoE scheme.

Many people have helped me in the production of this book. I have thanked those that helped me with the initial project in "My Thanks to". However, a number of people have assisted me in the publishing of this book. I am grateful to the sponsors: The Nestlé Company Ltd (Mr R J Banister), Coopers & Lybrand Deloitte (Mr Stuart McPherson) and the Croydon DoE Committee (Ms Jackie Harford). In addition, I would like to thank in particular Mr Clive Gronow and Ms Jan Davies of H & G Engineering. Jan magically transformed my hand-drawn sketch plans using a computer graphics package. I would also like to thank JEC Potter & Sons Ltd who have helped to typeset this book. I am grateful to Mr Colin Renwick and Mr Paul Hennessey, both of whom gave the publication of this book their utmost priority.

Also, I would like to thank Eyre & Spottiswoode Ltd. (Mr Roy Skinner), Robert Horne Paper Company Ltd, Olivers Paper Limited, CK Litho Ltd, Cedric Chivers Ltd and PROMT-CM Services for sponsoring some of the aspects of printing and publication of this book.

I gratefully acknowledge the kind permission given by the Rev R J Miller, Selworthy Church, the Rev Prebendary C H Saralis, Minehead Church and Mr B Williams, St Mary's in Oare, to reproduce their church sketch, plan and photograph, respectively.

Finally, I must thank HRH Prince Edward for his generous foreword, Mr Bernard Weatherill, MP, the Speaker of the House of Commons for a special introduction, Cllr, Jim Walker, Mayor of Croydon, for his introduction to the DoE Award Section, Mr Michael Hobbs CBE, Director of the Duke of Edinburgh's Award Scheme for all his help and last, but not least, my family for all their support.

Sharmila S Prabhu

Introduction

This project is for the Duke of Edinburgh (DOE) Award Scheme and in particular for the Expedition Section of the Gold Award. The DOE Award requirements for this section states (and I quote):

> "Explorations
>
> At least ten hours are to be spent journeying in wild or open country. The remaining hours of planned activity are to be spent on:
>
> (a) when camping, the pitching and striking of tents (approximately one hour per overnight camp).
>
> and (b) first hand observations and enquiries, eg natural geographical or historical surveys.
>
> or (c) physical activities such as orienteering, climbing or caving."

I chose Exmoor for a number of reasons. Firstly, when I started planning the exploration, Exmoor was considered by the Awards Board as wild country and at the Gold Award level, the Expedition Section usually takes place in such areas. Secondly, having seen the beautiful countryside during a Gold practice journey in 1986, I wanted to go back and explore the area in general but in particular, the ancient and historical churches, to a greater extent. During the practice journey, I came across and also heard about a number of small villages around Exmoor that were worth exploring in detail. All this was made possible when I decided upon local churches as the subject of my project/survey.

For my Bronze DOE Award, I also chose churches for a project on its Expedition Section. Those churches were situated in an area of 15-20 square miles in the Dorking area in Surrey. I found a notable difference between these churches and those around Exmoor, namely their age. They were more like the churches in Minehead that I have included in the Appendix, ie they were of more recent times than those scattered around Exmoor.

Each church included in the main part of the project, except the Church of St Mary the Virgin, Oare, and those in Minehead, has a photograph* and a rough sketch plan (not to scale). Unfortunately, the print of the church in Oare was not developed clearly hence a photocopy of a picture found in a leaflet is used. The information for this project was collected by first-hand observations of the churches during planned walks and was supplemented by details from leaflets and some historical notes displayed in the churches. A Bibliography follows the Glossary section. I found the book 'The Buildings of England - South and West Somerset' by N Pevsner particularly useful.

The Appendix includes three churches, mainly Methodist, which were closed, therefore no information could be gathered but photographs were taken and so they have been included. Also in the Appendix are three churches that I came across in Minehead which I have included so that they can be compared with those in the countryside.

Throughout the project, words or phrases associated with architecture or with church matters are typed in *italics*. These are defined in the Glossary section at the end of the project.

Projects for DOE Expeditions are usually produced by a group, but, as I was the only person to be assessed, the whole project is my own work. This project covers Part (b) of the above mentioned DOE Award requirements. Part (a) has been assessed and signed by the Assistant District Commissioner for West Somerset.

Sharmila S. Prabhu

* I took all the photographs using my own camera and would like to apologise to the reader for their quality.

Exmoor

Exmoor is an extensive area (265 square miles) of moorland which is a National Park. The Park straddles the West Somerset and North Devon borders. It stretches north, from Foreland Point, southwards to Brushford, east from Monksilver, westwards to Combe Martin and ranging in height from sea level, in the north, to 519m above sea level (Dunkery Beacon). Hence, Exmoor towers over the Bristol Channel, its magnificent coastline hogsback headlands giving a superb view across to the distant Welsh mountains.

The open expanse has either heather or purple moor grass as the dominating plant and the lower parts of the valleys are often thickly covered with oak woods. Clear streams run fast in the valleys, many of which join up, in the south to form the Rivers Barle and Exe and in the north the East and West Lyn.

On the whole, the only people to have lived on top of the moor have been those who have had their work cut out farming, or, until the turn of the century, mining. Not much remains of the latter but you can still see isolated, sturdy farms, often still with their sheltering trees and surrounded by a few fields. Hedges of small beech trees planted along the top of huge stone and earth banks, often running for miles, are barriers against the all too common wind, rain and snow.

Most of the villages and towns nestle into the valleys which have the shelter and comfort that the moor so much lacks. Even along the coast, where high cliffs drop into the sea, the settlements have mostly grown up where the cliff line is broken.

The low-lying farmland is divided into fields (mostly cultivated pasture) and the emphasis is on sheep with some beef cattle. The local breed of sheep, the Exmoor Horn, is one of three animals specially associated with Exmoor, the others being the Exmoor Pony and the animal that has been adopted as the emblem of the National Park, the Red Deer. The large bird often seen flying above is the Buzzard, now common again as rabbit numbers have increased.

Map of Exmoor

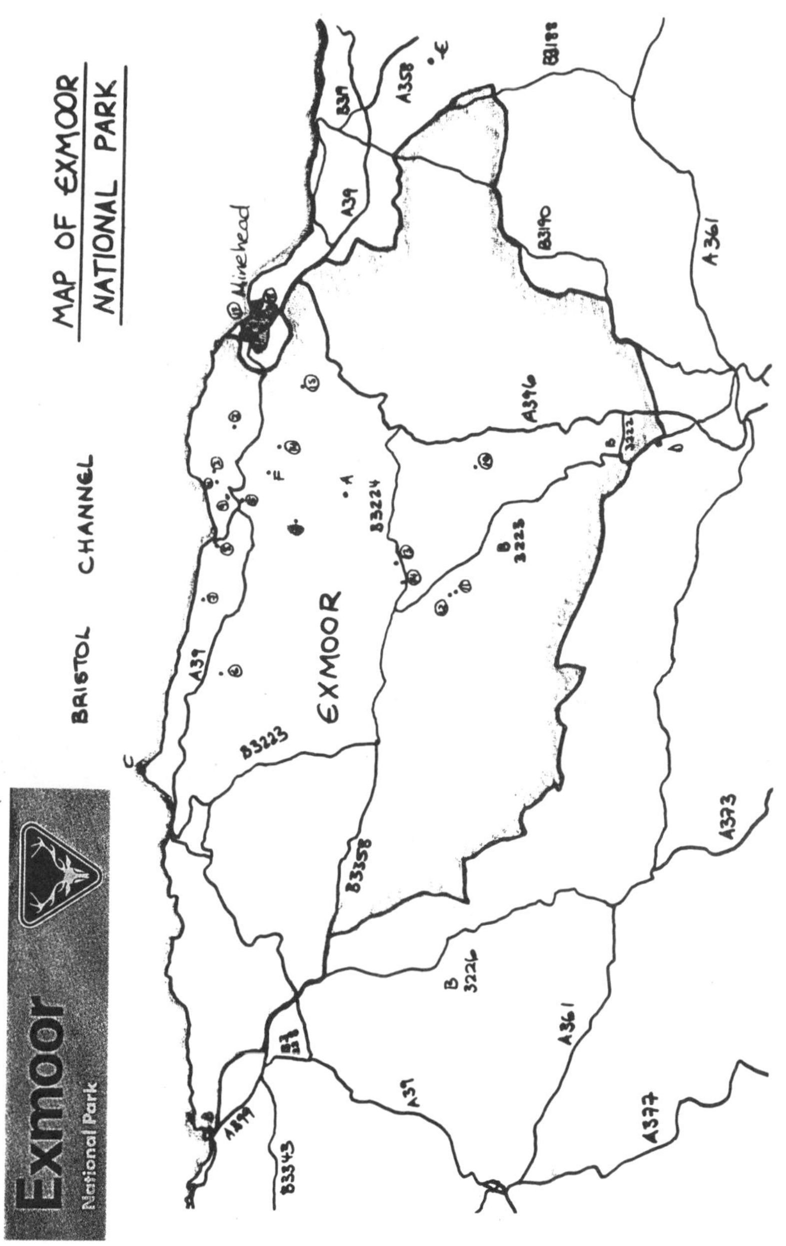

Plan of Exmoor

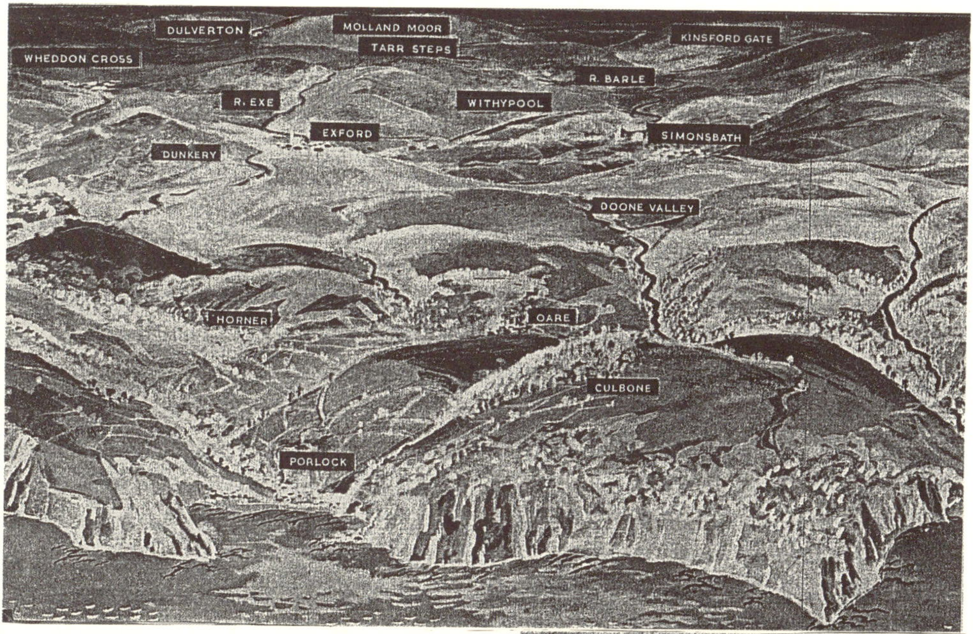

Church Layout in General

Most churches have a few basic things in common. For example, churches in general (except Methodist) face east, ie the *altars* are at the east end of the church. They all have an altar and *nave*, *chancel*, some also have *aisles*, *arcades*, a bell tower, a porch, etc.

The plan shown opposite outlines the parts of a typical church.

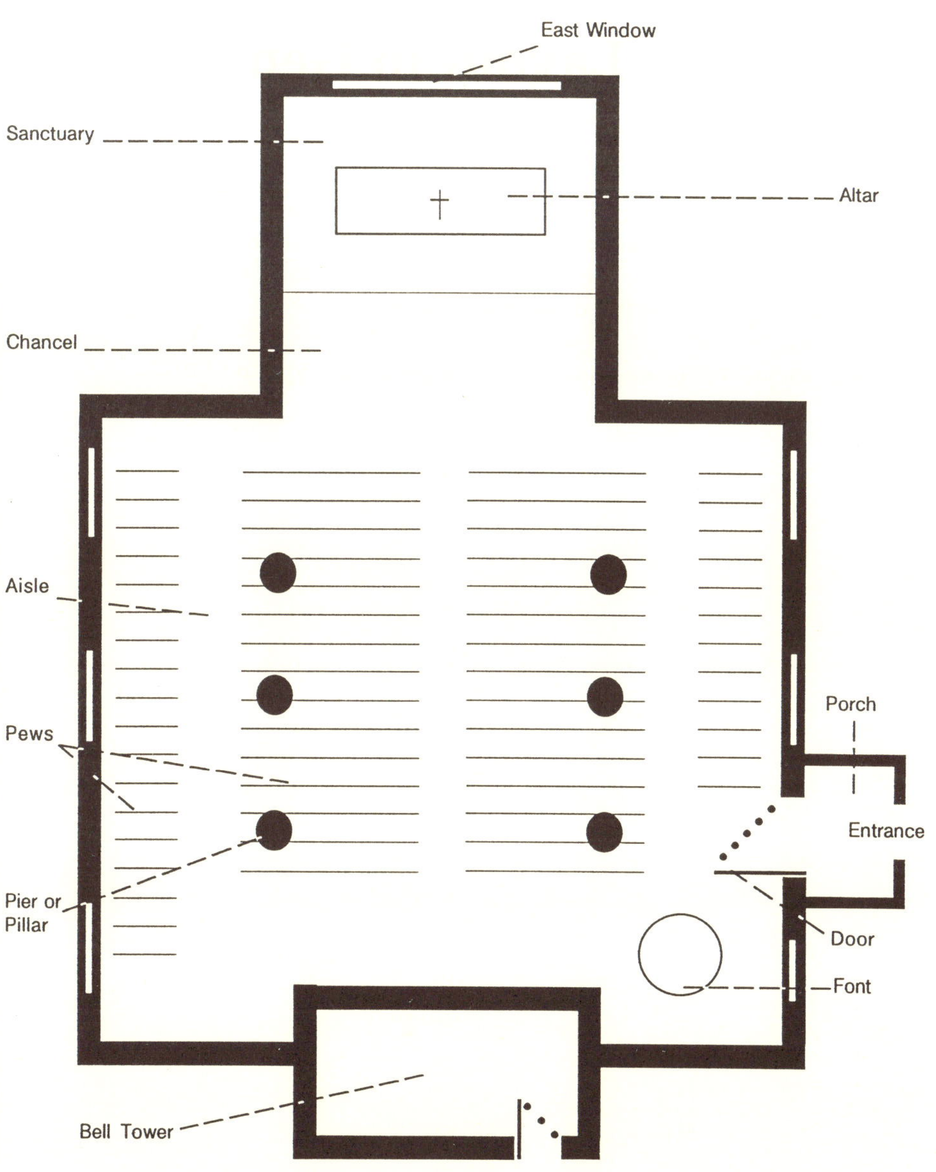

Plan of a Typical Church

Church of St Mary the Virgin, Oare
Drawing by Rev Donald Flatt (Reproduced with kind permission)

Churches on Exmoor

St Peter's Church, Stoke Pero

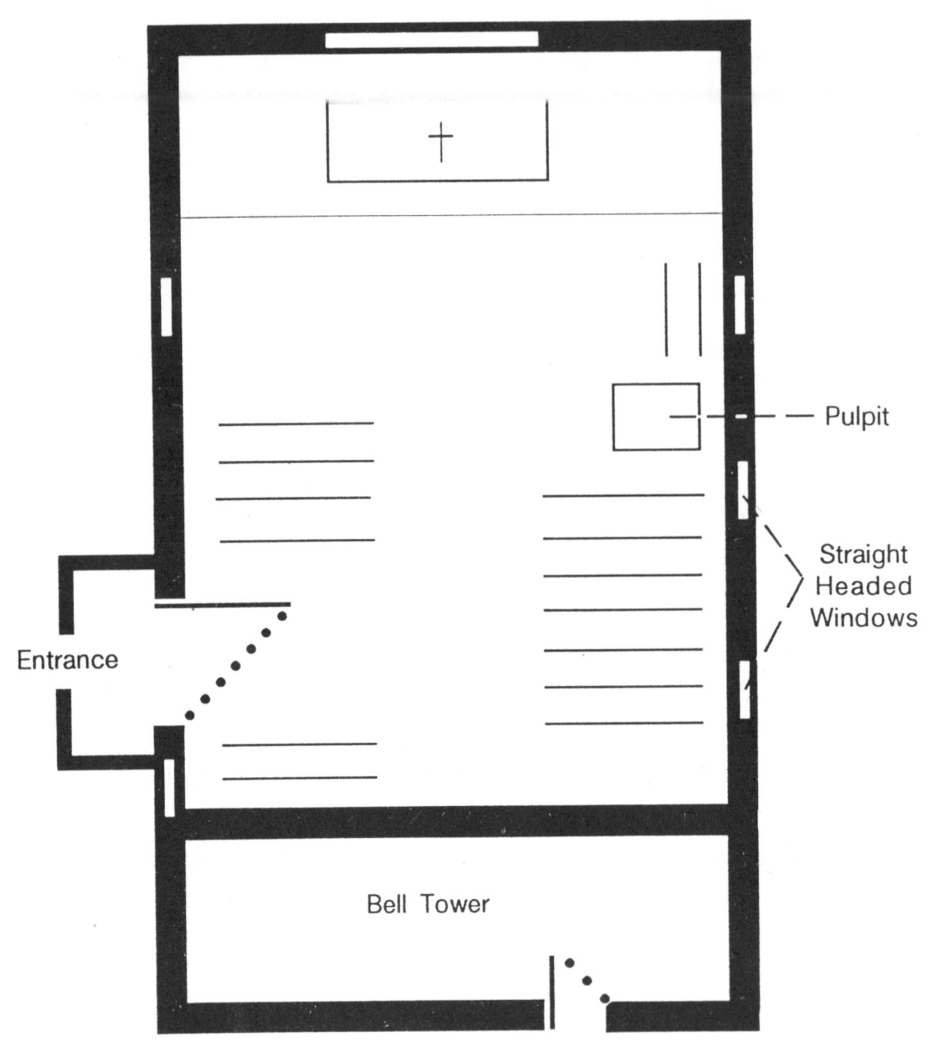

Plan of St Peter's Church, Stoke Pero

St Peter's Church, Stoke Pero

Except for one whitewashed farmhouse, St Peter's Church, Stoke Pero, stands all alone on Exmoor. It must be one of the most solitary churches in Somerset. The inscription on the front gate reads:

> "Stoke Pero Parish Church. (Mentioned in Domes Day Book).
> The most isolated and highest church on Exmoor.
> 1013 feet above sea level"

There is an old rhyme which emphasises its loneliness:

> "Culbone, Oare and Stoke Pero
> Parishes three, no parson'll go to.
>
> Culbone, Oare and Stoke Pero
> Three such places you'll seldom hear o'."

Stoke Pero is said to be the earliest Christian site on Exmoor but the date and even the dedication of the church are lost. It has been suggested that the inscription 'sancts barbara' on the fifteenth century bell might be a memory of the original dedication. St Barbara was the patron saint of miners in France. It is not very clear as to the link between a French miner's saint and this remote Exmoor church.

The church is set in a hollow so deep that the top of its tower seems level with the rim of a bowl. The west tower is of only one stage and a bit but was probably meant to go up higher. There is a tower arch on the most simplest of *imposts* suggesting possibly Norman workmanship or that of a very simple-minded workman. The church was rebuilt in 1897 - the earlier structure was left in ruins. The wooden door, some window frames and stones of medieval times have been incorporated in the present building. St Peter was given an excellent *saddleback barrel-beamed roof* for which the timber was transported from Porlock by a donkey, Zulu!

The church was restored again in 1958. It has a *nave* and *chancel* with *straight-headed windows*. The interior is white thereby stressing its solitude rather than its antiquity. Yet the *chalice* and *paten* (Barnstable-made) have been in use since 1574 and the first known incumbent (someone holding an office in a church) was instituted in 1242.

All Saints' Church, Selworthy

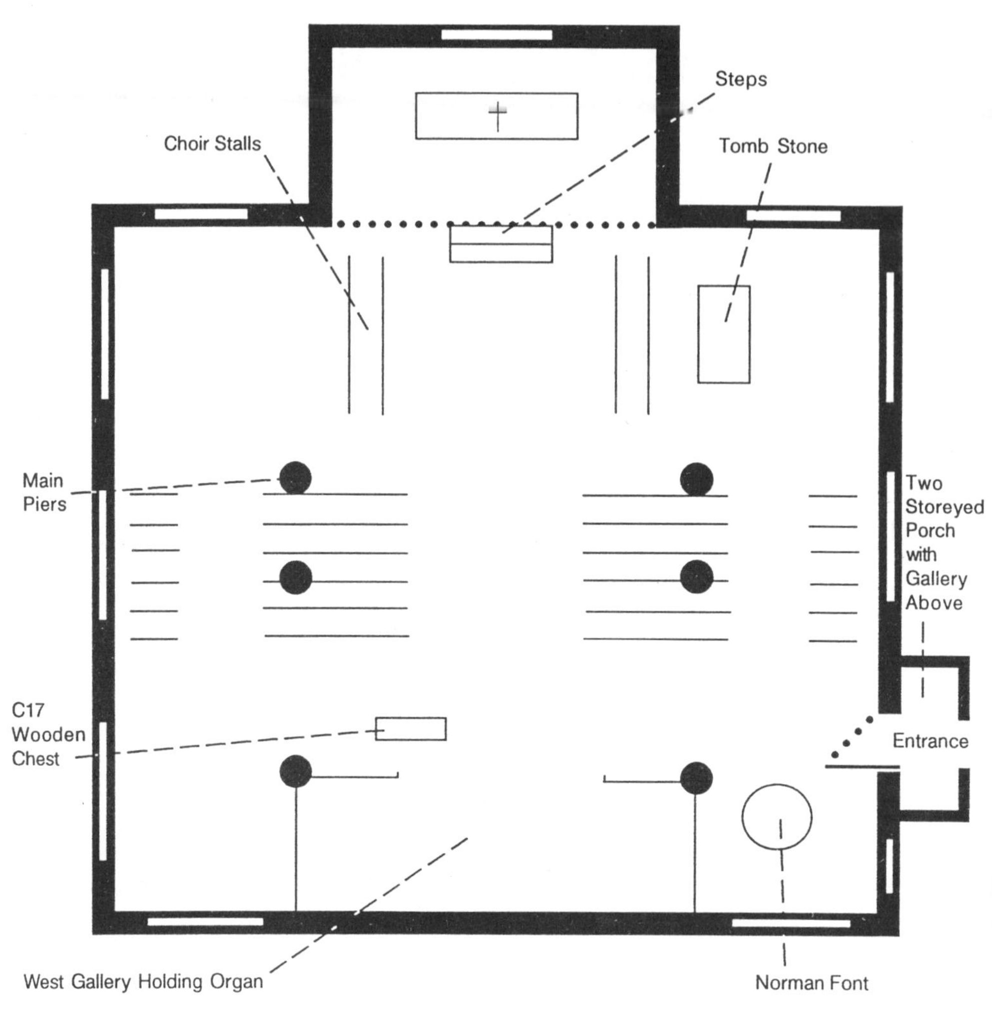

Plan of All Saints' Church, Selworthy

All Saints' Church, Selworthy

The building consists of a *chancel*, a *nave*, north and south *aisles*, a west tower and a south porch. In architecture and situation the church is one of the most attractive in the country. The severity of the winter storms is acknowledged by the church council in continuing to coat the exterior of the church with a mix of lime and tallow (white in colour hence making it visible for many miles) for protection against the driving rain. This is the only church on Exmoor to be shielded in this way.

The interior of All Saints is airy with tall slim *piers* and large windows. It has *four-bay arcades* and piers with *four-waves section*. The *capitals* are partly very crisply modelled leaf bands and partly small polygons for the four shafts only. Portions of the existing chancel walls belong to an earlier church comprising of a chancel and nave to which, in the latter part of the fourteenth century, the tower was added (the only exception to the otherwise Perpendicular church). The tombstone in the *chancel* is typical of the *Perpendicular* structure surrounding it, with no *effigies*. The communion rail made around 1700 has quite slim turned *balusters*. The *paten* (of possibly Dutch origin), styled domestically, was made in the seventeenth century as was the *chalice*. Amongst the church's treasures are sixteenth century candlesticks and a 1760 *flagon*. Preaching takes place from a restored sixteenth century *pulpit*.

The *embattled* south front has a *three-light* and a *four-light window* separated by a two-storeyed south porch with a doorway finely panelled up the *jambs* and along the arch. The Holnicote family had a delightful little *pavilion* in the *parvise* chamber of the porch. The porch contains the remains of a Holy Water *stoup*. Just inside the door into the nave is the Norman *font*. The *tracery* of the large, *transomed*, south windows is of that exquisite, but by no means exuberant design worked out probably at Dunster or Watchet and used at Cleeve Abbey or Luccombe. The beautiful south aisle, one of the treasures of the Church of England, is dated 1538. Its exceptionally fine *wagon-roof*, perpendicular window and arcade are of unquestionable grace and proportion. The roof has richly decorated plates with angels holding shields, *braces*, *purlins* and large *bosses* with faces of Christ and the Symbols of the Passion etc.

The north *aisle* is plainer and was probably built earlier. The east window of the north *aisle* is a similar type to those on the south front, but it contains fragments of old stained glass. The *chancel* east window is probably a little earlier. The west gallery, on *Doric pilasters* carrying a *metope frieze*, on which the organ has now been placed is of good classical work and was erected in 1750. There is a seventeenth century chest made from a single elm strongly bound with iron bands and three locks which was used to safekeep the church's treasures when they were not required for the services. A key to each lock was given to three different men so that no one man could have access to the chest's priceless contents.

Lynch Chapel, Lynch

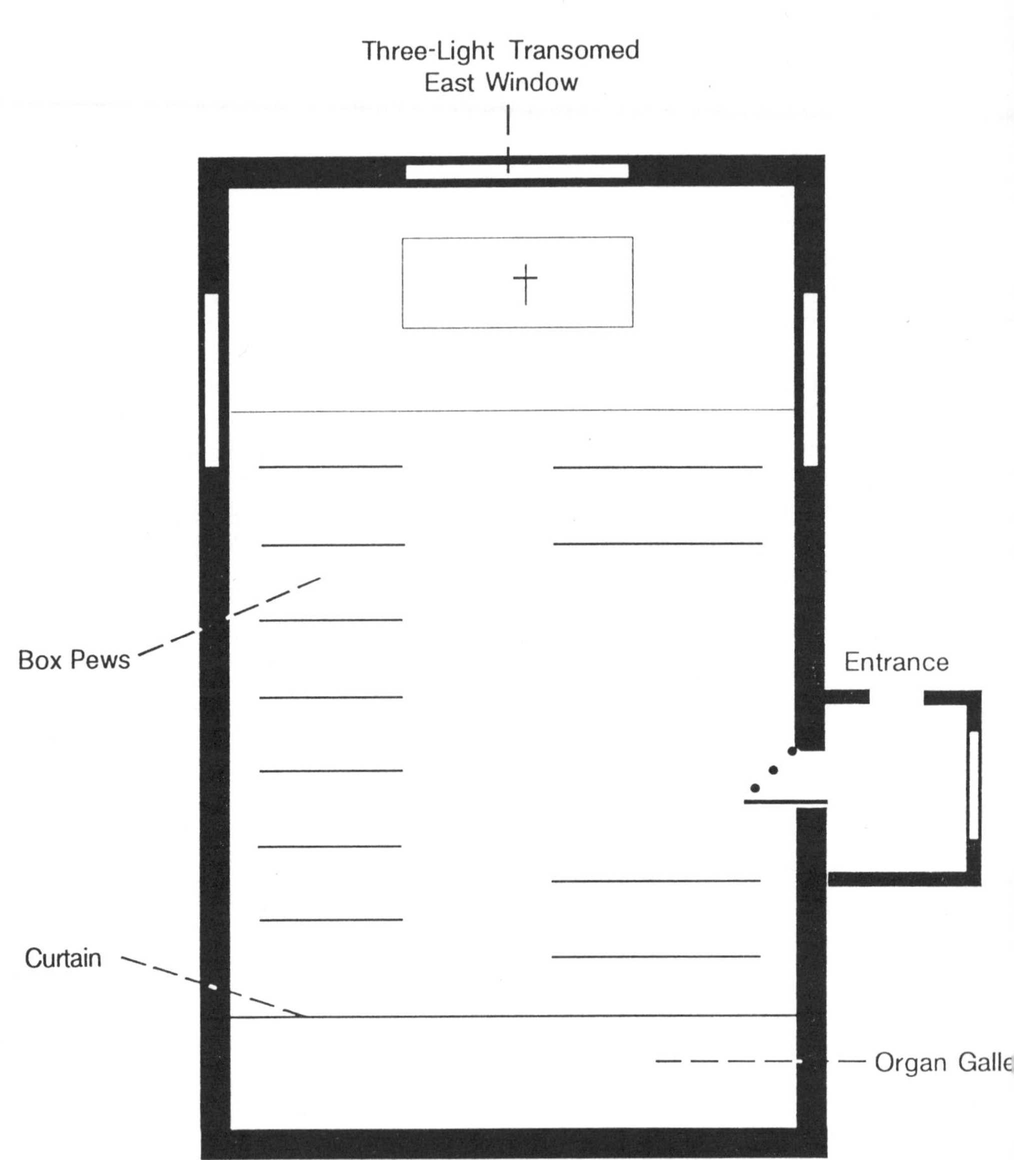

Plan of Lynch Chapel, Lynch

Lynch Chapel, Lynch

Lynch Chapel is a sixteenth century *chapel*. The unusually ambitious *three-light, transomed* east window (not the sort of window found in a manor house *chapel*), crafted by Mr Christopher Webb, records briefly the history of the Manor of Bossington, of which it is the *chapel*.

Lynch Chapel-of-Ease was probably built about 1530, at the same time as the south *aisle* of the parish church of Selworthy. It is thought that it was a memorial *chapel* of the Manor of Bossington which had been in the possession of Athelney Abbey since 920 AD. After the Dissolution of the Monasteries in the 1500's the *chapel* fell into disuse and was used as a barn. It was restored in 1885 by Sir Thomas Acland and has been used regularly for services ever since.

The *two-light* north and south windows are original, but the *tracery* of the east window had to be rebuilt. The *wagon-roof* is ancient and eleven of the original *bosses* still remain. A second restoration took place in 1930. The organ-gallery was built at this time. Some of the wood from the old *box-pews* in All Saints church, Selworthy, which were removed in 1875, was used for this and the panelled *dado*. A porch has been built recently to protect the old door. The door has an old wooden bolt in the wall by the latch.

St Dubricius Church, Porlock

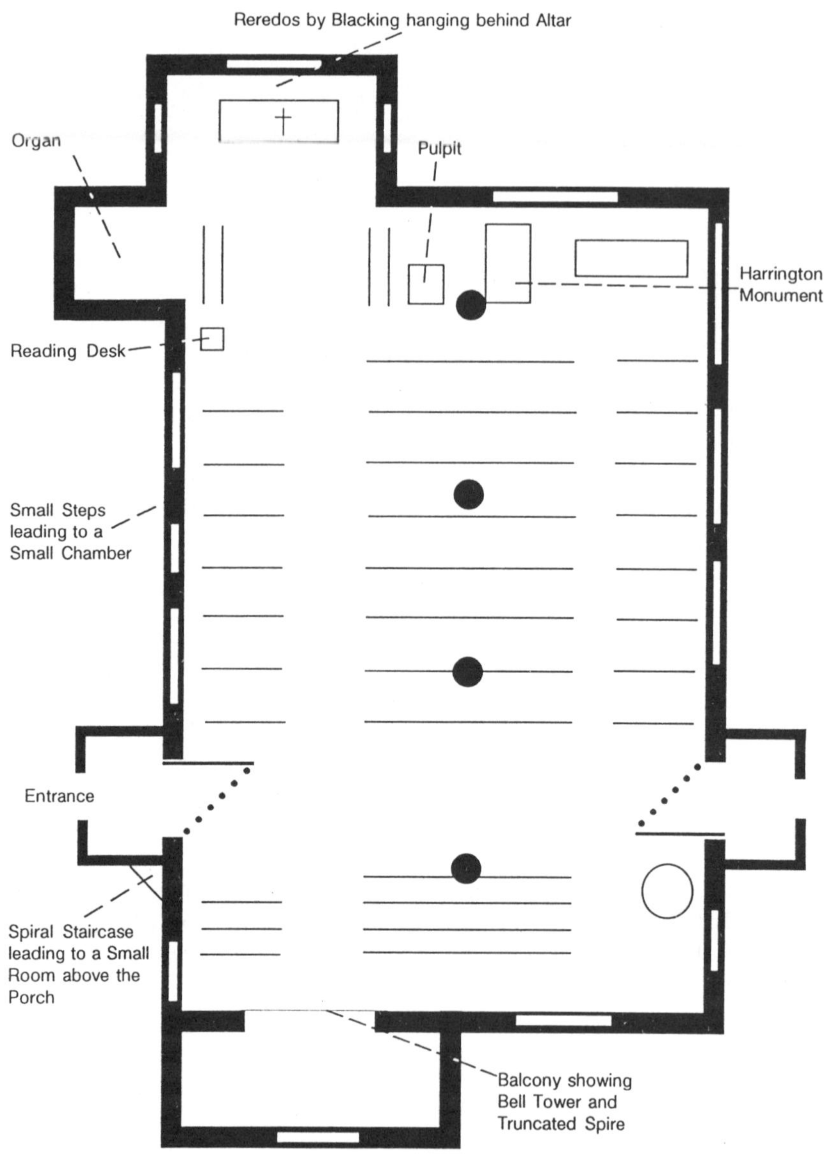

Plan of St Dubricius Church, Porlock

St Dubricius Church, Porlock

St Dubricius lived between 500-600 AD. He was a Welsh saint who was said to have recrowned King Arthur. He founded a church in Porlock. The first stone church was built about 1100 and the present building dates from the thirteenth century, being reconstructed around 1400-1500. The *Living* is in the gift of the crown since Elizabeth I. The first recorded rector was in 1297. In May 1642, Charles I presented the Living to Dr Adam Bellenden, Bishop of Aberdeen. There is some reason to think that he brought with him a member of the Dourne family who lived near Perth and here is to be found the beginnings of the Doone Legends which R D Blackmore used so vividly in 'Lorna Doone'.

St Dubricius church has a low heavy thirteenth century west tower with a singled *spine*. This truncated *spine* is Porlock's trademark. Tradition says that the missing top was damaged in a gale in 1703 and never replaced. But old residents have other explanations. One is that when the spine was nearly finished a hunt passed through Porlock. The workman came down and never returned to complete the work. Others say that the 1703 gale removed the top in one piece and blew it over the hills and woods to Culbone, where it settled on the roof of the church and is there to this day! It was restored in 1884 and again in 1933. There are six bells contained in the tower, three of which date back to 1617. The *tower arch* leads towards the *nave* with one slight *chamfer*.

The building has a *nave*, *chancel* with original east *vestry* and south *aisle*. The main entrance is through the two-storeyed north porch essentially fifteenth century but additions were made around 1890. Inside the late fourteenth century south *arcade* of five *bays* and octagonal *piers*, there are very elementary shaped *capitals* and *double-chamfered* arches. Under the fifth arch of the arcade is the Harrington monument (not in its original position). The *tomb-chest* has many small niches and a tall *canopy* with *fleurons* up the *jambs* and along the *four-centred* arch. In the *spandrels* is a *cusped* arch *tracery*. On the *tomb-*

chest lie the alabaster *effigies* of Lord John Harrington (died 1418, Lord of the Manor of Porlock) and his wife, of good quality and dating from about 1460. Once richly coloured, they are of the finest of their kind in England. The *effigies* have suffered mutilation and are defaced with initials, some dated as early as 1690. The *effigy* of Harrington's wife has beautiful rounded folds to the lower part of her dress on top of which lies a small stone boar. The monument still retains traces of colours.

There is another *tomb-chest*, in the *chancel*, with *quatrefoils* and without effigies, which is known as the Easter Tomb. It is so called because the *altar crucifix* and *holy vessels* were hidden there on Good Friday and 'found' on Easter Monday symbolising the death and resurrection of Christ. A third tomb lies in the south porch and a fourth in the north porch. The latter is a large early *Perpendicular font* tomb removed from the churchyard and made from Dundry (Somerset) stone. In a recess of the south *aisle* lies the damaged remains of an *effigy* of a Knight in Chain Armour. The thirteenth century knight is said to represent a certain Sir Simon Fitz Roges. The small steps in the north wall, which led to a chamber over the *rood screen*, were removed in 1769.

Behind the *altar* hangs a *reredos* by W H R Blacking in the style of Voysey*. On the altar stands a 1727 dish and a *chalice* of possibly Elizabethan times. Most of the windows in the *chancel* and elsewhere are plain except for large panels of glass set in pale coloured flowers, their outlines formed by the leading of the glass. They were crafted in 1890.

Probably the most precious relic of the past and possibly the earliest Christian monument in West Somerset or North Devon, that is after the stone on Winsford Hill, is the Saxon Cross on the wall at the west end of the church. Under the west tower arch, on the *nave* side, stands the ancient clock which was made around 1400-1450. It had no face or hands but rang the hours on the tenor bell in the tower. It was still

* One of the best domestic architects of England, worked around 1900.

working up to the time of Queen Victoria's jubilee. The stone weights, on the clock, are the original ones.

Over the north porch is room for the use of the monks and served the Harrington *chantry* (1475-1546). The monks lived in a cottage in the 'Drang', a lane near the church. It is still known as Chantry Cottage.

Church of St Mary the Virgin, Oare

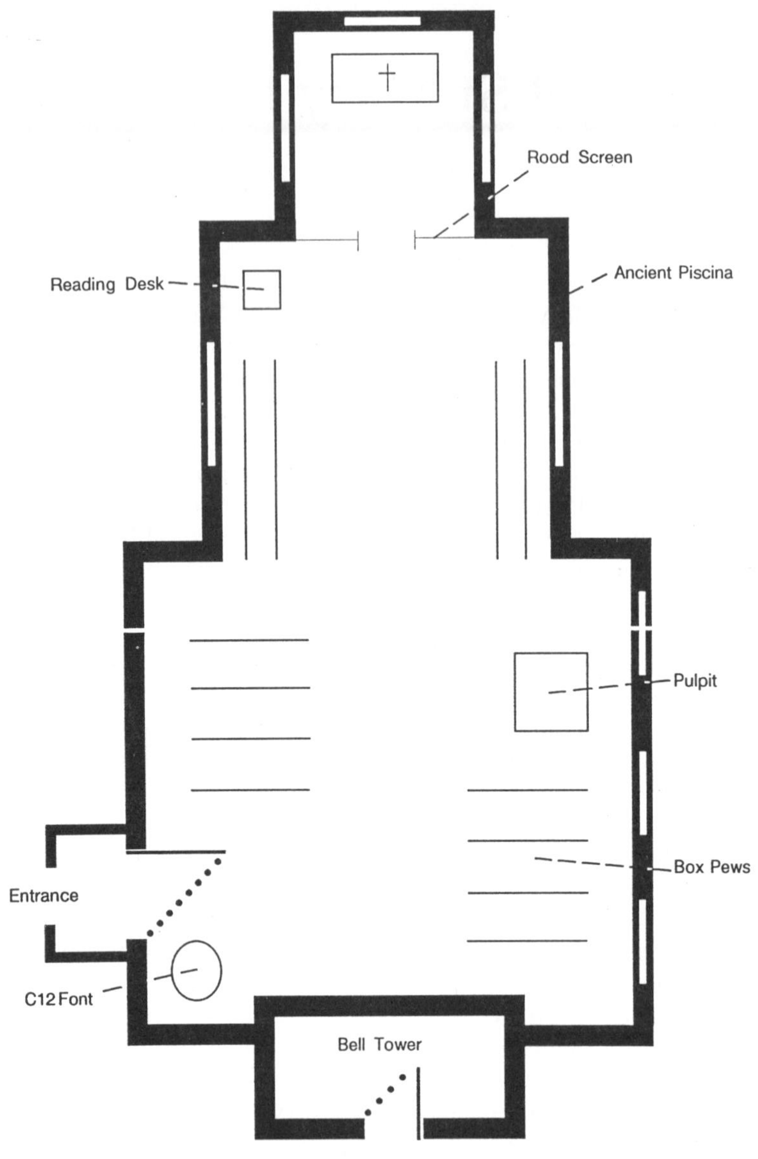

Plan of the Church of St Mary the Virgin, Oare

Church of St Mary the Virgin, Oare

The Church of St Mary the Virgin is a small plain building with a low square tower at the west end blending in very well with its moorland surroundings. It is on the site of an Anglo-Saxon settlement called Are.

For at least 800 years this building has been a parish church. The roofs of the *nave* and inner (or old) *chancel* are of the *wagon* type, and are probably of the fifteenth century. The ceiling is covered in white plaster to lighten the interior. The *nave* is a remarkably good and untouched example of the treatment of Georgian times. It is lit by three square *domestic-looking* windows on the south side.

On the south side of the inner *chancel* is a *piscina* in the shape of a head (probably meant to represent St Decuman); it indicated that the *altar* stood there until modern times, west of the position of the present screen. The east window, therefore, is also modern in comparison to the inner *chancel*. The *chancel* was lengthened in the mid-nineteenth century, when the west tower was rebuilt. On the present *altar* stands a *chalice* dated 1573, a *flagon* and *paten* both from 1802 and an *almsdish* of 1813.

Entry to this church is through a north porch and an oaken doorway. The porch, as with many old churches, is a relatively new addition to protect the old door. On the immediate right when coming through the door stands a *font* whose basin may be at least as old as the twelfth century. The octagonal base and the stem of the *font* are comparatively modern, very likely early nineteenth century. Parishioners sit in *box pews*, made at the same time as the *pulpit* and *reading desk*, late eighteenth or early nineteenth century. At the back of the church is the west tower, as mentioned above, with three bells cast in 1873. The old bell (dated 1770) is also preserved for the clock to strike upon. Thomas Bayley, a Bridgewater bell-founder, cast this bell. He has engraved his name on it with the motto 'Memento mori'.

Behind the *font*, on the north wall, hangs a memorial to Richard Doddridge Blackmore, a reproduction of one which hangs in Exeter Cathedral. Richard Blackmore was the famous author of 'Lorna Doone', a tragic romance set in the surrounding countryside (a nearby valley is named Doone Valley) in the late seventeenth century. Lorna's life was brought to a sudden end when Carver Doone shot her through a church window during her wedding service. The incident is described in the book as follows:

> "The sound of a shot rang out through the church, and those eyes were dim with death. Lorna fell across my knees, when I was going to kiss her as a bridegroom is allowed to do, and encouraged, if he needs it; a flood of blood came out upon the yellow wood of the altar step, and at my feet fell Lorna"

The window through which Carver shot Lorna is one of the single windows which still remains at the sides of the inner *chancel* west of the screen. The church, then as mentioned above, ended where the screen now stands. In those days the *box-pews* were open benches and the *chancel* roof had *ribs* and *bosses*, some of which are preserved under the *chancel* arch. Richard Blackmore's grandfather, John Blackmore, was a Rector of Oare from 1809 to 1842, although the parish records suggest that he rarely (if at all) came to Oare. A possible member of the Ridd family, mentioned in 'Lorna Doone', was a churchwarden as recently as 1914-25. His grandson, David Richards, now holds this office.

St Beuno Church, Culbone

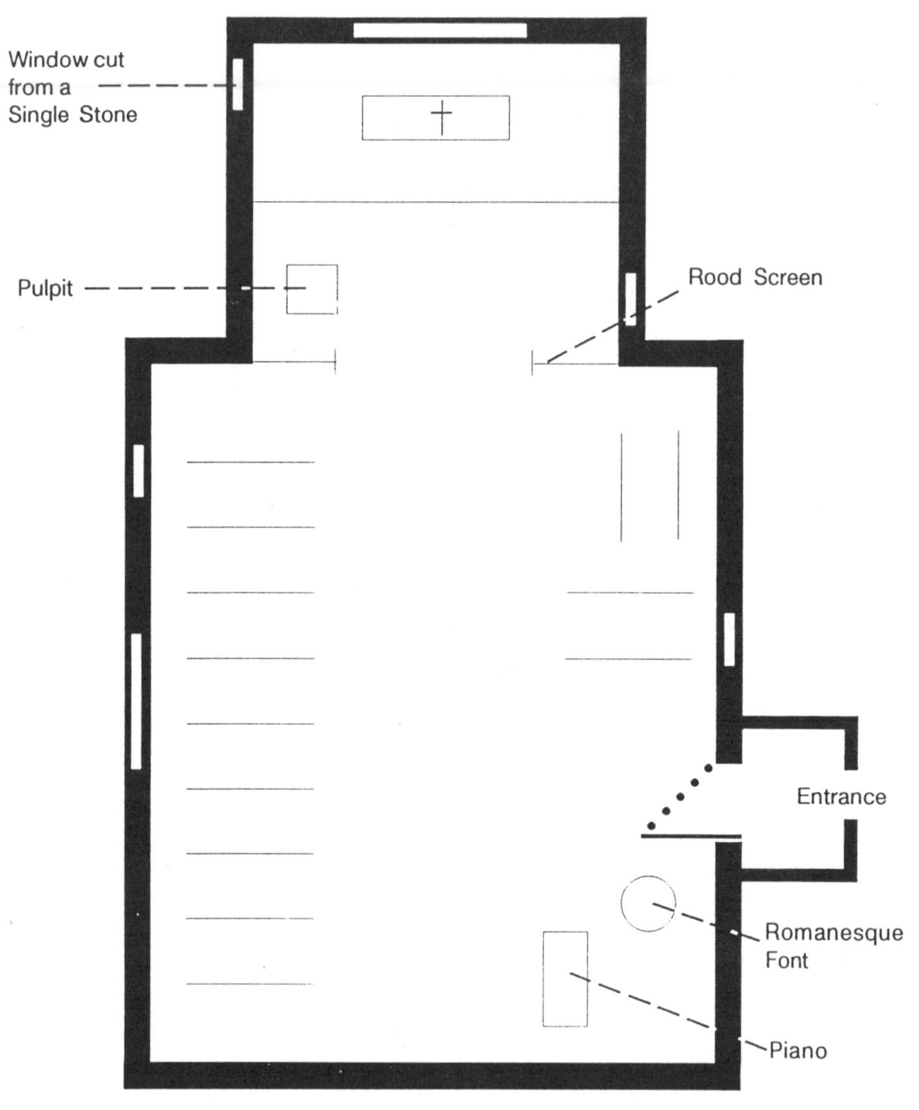

Plan of St Beuno Church, Culbone

St Beuno Church, Culbone

St Beuno was a seventeenth century saint of Wales, whilst Culbone means the cell of Beuno. One would not imagine St Beuno Church to be mentioned in the Guinness Book of Records but the quote reads:

> "The smallest completed medieval English church in regular use is that at Culbone, Somerset, which measures 35 x 12ft (10.66 x 3.65m)."

St Beuno is isolated by a rushing stream and wooded hillside rising 800 feet above. Culbone was long known as Kitnor - cave by the shore. The only access is by foot along winding tracks that curl down the cliffs through the woods. It is a tiny church, as the measurements show, with a little slate *spire* (of 1810) riding on the west end of the *nave* roof. The whitewash on the interior has come off in irregular patches to expose *rubble* underneath explained by the church's Norman origins, although the present walls are known to be of the twelfth century and other parts of the building are Saxon. Remains of Norman masonry can be found in the *chancel.*

Entry to St Beuno is via a *gabled* porch into a small slated *nave.* On the left-hand side of the door in the *nave* stands a Romanesque *font.* This west side also houses two bells under the *spire*, one of which is the earliest found in West Somerset, dated probably from the early fourteenth century. On the north side there is fragmentary evidence of an *anchorite's* cell. Also on this wall the remains of a carved heads can be traced. The ceiling is plastered with *ribs* and carved *bosses*, the ceiling rail also being carved. The church-goers are now seated on *square headed* benches, completely plain (probably *pre-reformation).* There is a family pew, made in a very simple seventeenth century style.

The slated *chancel* is lit by a tiny *square-headed* leaded window which is the oldest feature of the church. It is pre-Norman and cut out of a single stone. The *chancel* is separated from the *nave* by a *rood-screen.* It is assigned to a date earlier than 1400. It consists of *one-light* sections supported by a heavy framework with *quartrefoiled* circles on *stilted cusped* round arches. The *mullions* have been unfortunately removed. On the altar stands a *chalice* and *cover* dated 1573. Behind these is the *reredos* which is by *Voysey* in 1928 and it is *non-Gothic* rather than in the earlier *Voysey* style. It replaced a clumsy Victorian erection. At the extreme east end of the *chancel* is the east window, unfortunately renewed to such a degree that it seems insensitive.

Despite its solitude and inaccessibility, St Beuno is in regular use, as the Guinness Book of Records states.

St Mary Magdalene, Winsford

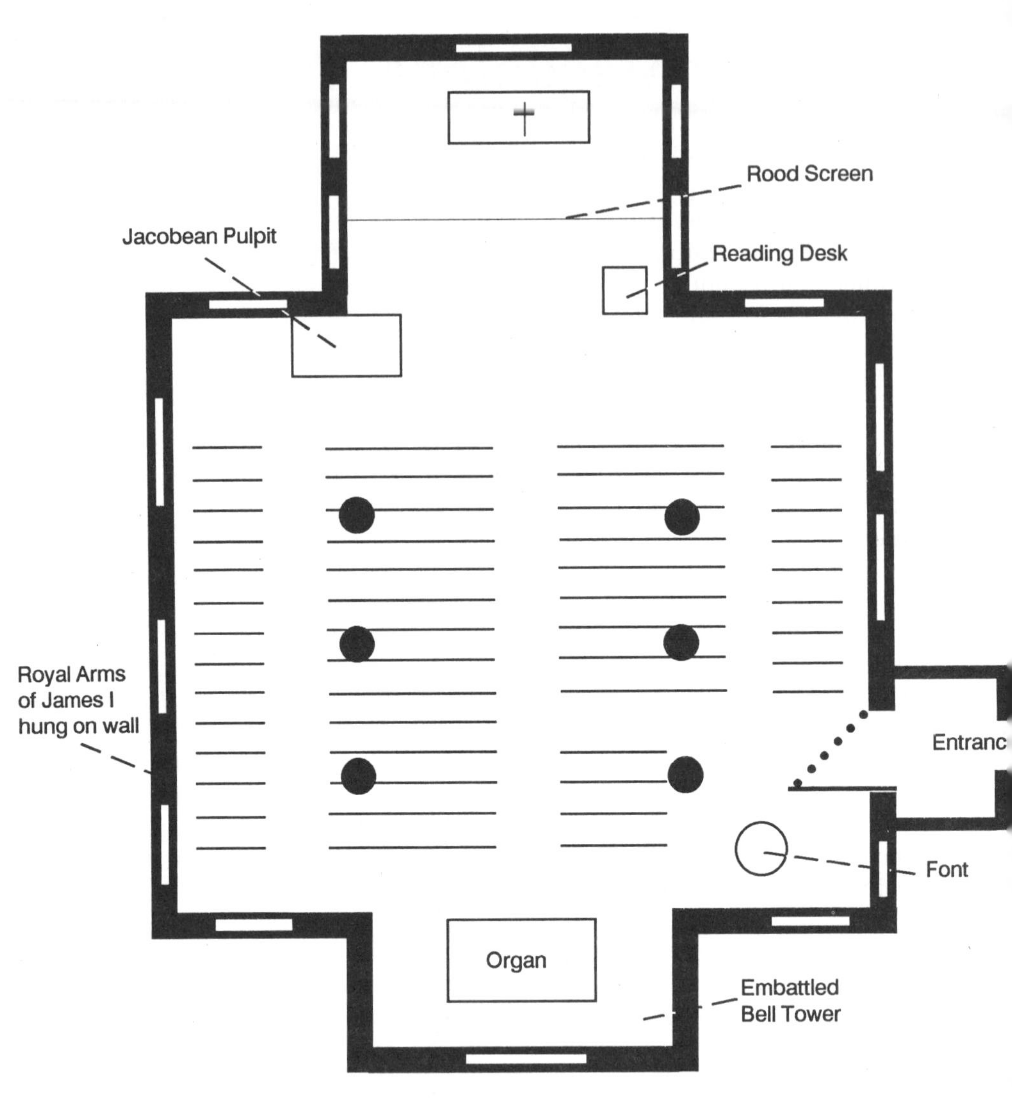

Plan of St Mary Magdalene, Winsford

St Mary Magdalene, Winsford

St Mary Magdalene, formerly dedicated to St Peter, is a *Perpendicular* hilltop church. The only exceptions to the *Gothic* structure is the round-arched south doorway, which could be Norman, and the thirteenth century *chalice* and *lancet windows.*

At the west end of the church stands a *three-stage embattled tower*, with no *pinnacles*, which is big for the district in which it stands - nearby churches mostly have a *two-stage* tower. The tower is supported by *set-back buttresses.* There is a high *stair-turret* up the tower with a statue-niche in the south exterior side just above the *square headed window.*

The Norman thirteenth century door, now protected by a porch, was made in very thick wood and heavy ironwork. On the left-hand side, whilst coming through the door into the *nave*, is a circular Norman *font* with coarse blank arches, their shafts plaited. A *saltire cross frieze* hangs above. Opposite this, on the north wall, hangs the Royal Arms of James I, dated 1609, whose colours are still bright due to the good condition in which it has been kept. The *Perpendicular nave* and *aisles* are under the same big roof externally. The *aisle arcades* of *four bays* have *piers* with *four-hollow standard* sections but which have been primitively treated. The pulpit is *Jacobean* with arches.

The *nave* is separated from the *chancel* by a *chancel arch* above. The latter has two windows, which is a rarity in this part of England. On the *altar* stands a 1574 *chalice* and a 1633 *paten,* the latter initialled with IM. The *chancel* east window is of the late *Perpendicular* period which is popular in the neighbourhood (eg Porlock, Exford). It has a *transom* and an *ogee arch* to each light beneath it. It also has a small figure of the Virgin in stained glass, probably made in the fourteenth century.

St Andrew's Chapel, Withypool

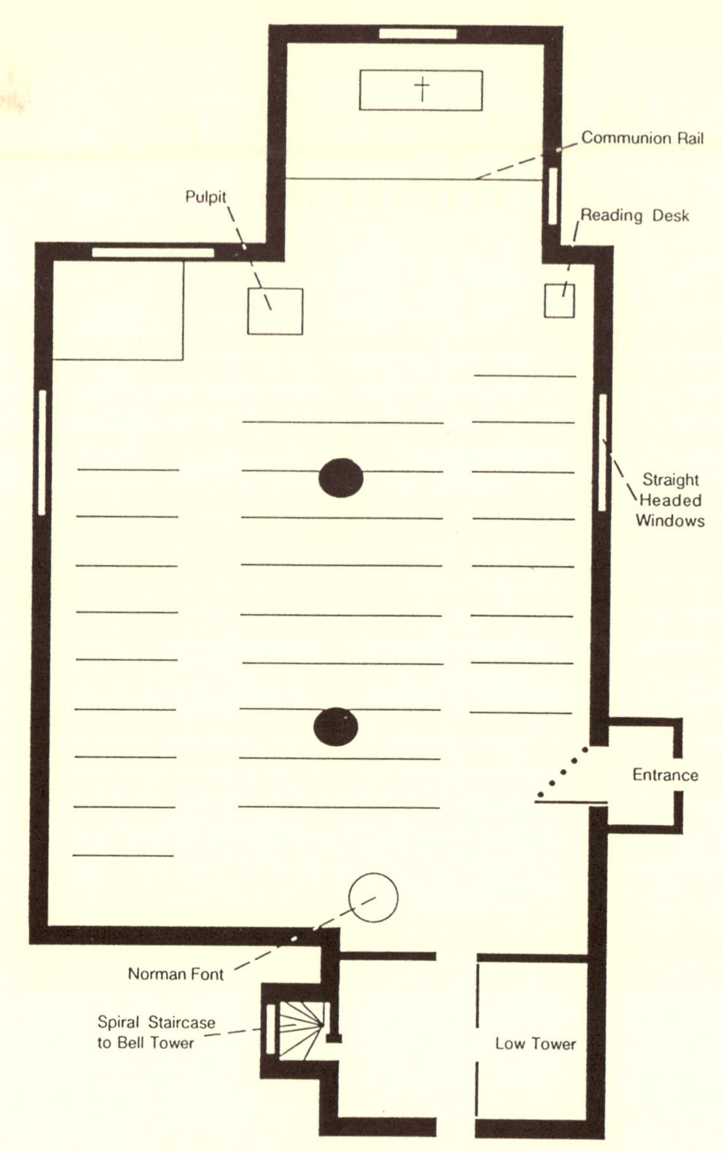

Plan of St Andrew's Chapel, Withypool

St Andrew's Chapel, Withypool

St Andrew's chapel has been largely rebuilt in 1901 leaving very little of the original church behind. Attempts were made to copy the old style but, as can be seen with the *tower arch* leading towards to the *nave*, there has been misinterpretation of the *Perpendicular* details.

At the west end of the *chapel* stands a low broad *two stage* tower, which is typical of the moorland churches. It has *embattlements* with *flying buttresses* but with no *pinnacles*. As with many churches in this region, a relatively new porch protects an older door. The interior of St Andrew's is painted white with a roof supported by wooden *rafters* without *bosses*.

The *nave* and rebuilt *chancel* are lit by *straight headed* windows. The *nave* consists of *aisles* with three-bay *arcades* supported by *piers* of *four-hollow sections*. The *capitals* of the *piers* have been reduced to a single moulding. Opposite the south door stands a Norman circular *font*, the bowl having a fluted underside and a band of parallel *chevrons*.

Under the east window stands a *chalice*, crafted in 1572 and initialled with IP, and a *paten*, made by a craftsman named Elston in 1726.

Methodist Church, Withypool

Methodist Church, Withypool

Although the Methodist church in Withypool no longer exists, the building still stands. It was known to be a very pretty little hall with a *Gothic ogee-arched* doorway and windows. It looked decidedly 1800 so the date of 1881 on a stone tablet which was laid in the church could not have been correct. Traces of carved stonework can be seen running along the corner of the building which could indicate the building's original use.

During the past thirty years the church has been converted into a private residence.

St Mary Magdalene, Exford

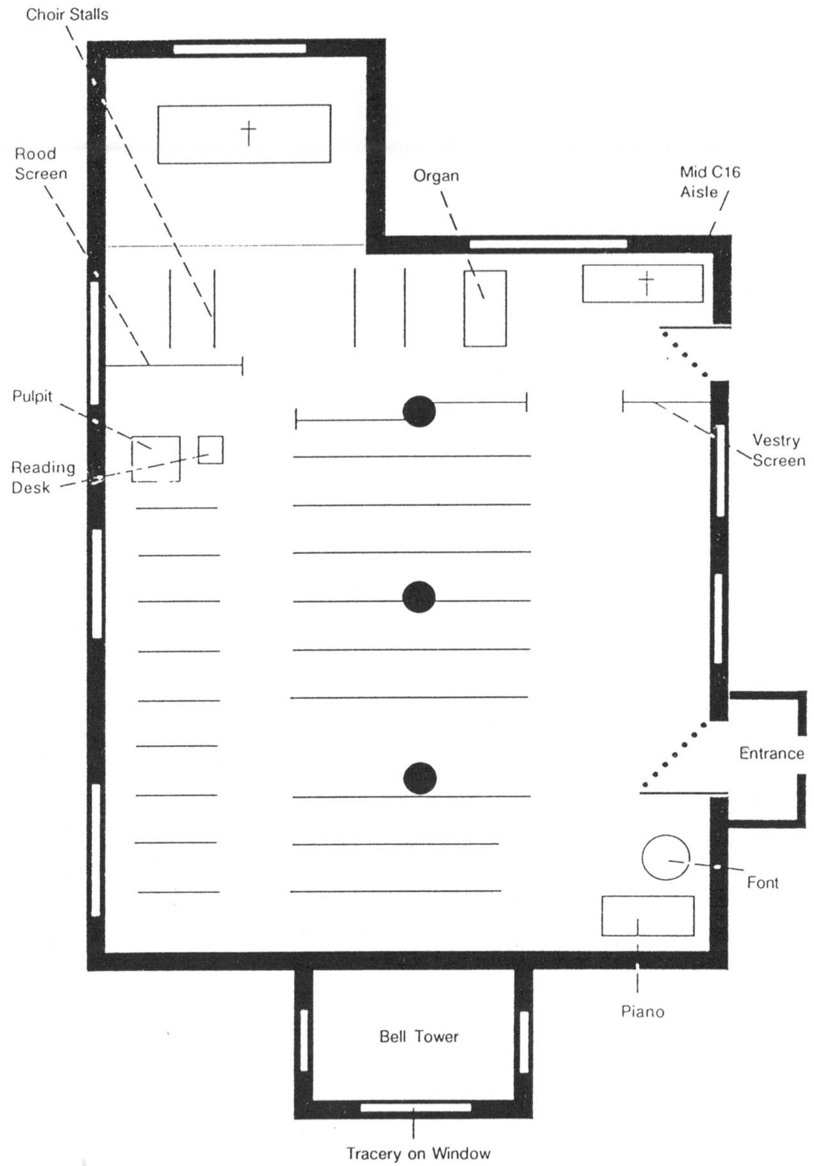

Plan of St Mary Magdalene, Exford

St Mary Magdalene, Exford

There has been a church on this ancient site since long before the Norman Conquest. Exford like Porlock, Culbone and others became the site of a church in the days when Christianity came to Somerset from Wales or Ireland and not from Roman mission which converted Saxon England. The church was dedicated to St Salvyn, a Celtic saint whose portrait with those of St George and Francis, is delineated in stained glass in the window on the east of the main door. The dedication to St Mary is of a much later date, the reason for which is rather obscure.

This church is of very ancient foundation although apart from the tower and the *arcades* there is very little early work left as it has been largely rebuilt more than once. In the Taunton Castle Museum there is a drawing of Exford church showing a *chancel* much lower and smaller than the *nave* - this must have been rebuilt later to the same height and width as the *nave.* The present building seems to be the third or fourth church on this site and historians believe that the foundations of the previous churches may still be found below the floor of the present *nave.*

The oldest part of the present church is the tower which dates from mid-fifteenth century. It is a plain, *embattled three stage tower*, which like Winsford, is unusual for such an exposed area. It is supported by *diagonal buttresses* and has a high *stair turret.* On the top corners of the tower are some quaint *gargoyles* which may originally have been intended as rain spouts but were not hollowed out. The west window has a *Perpendicular tracery;* the *label terminals,* although rough, are very striking. On the south side of the *tracery* is an angel holding a shield, whilst on the north side a demon stands. Above the top of the window is an angel holding a shield bearing three *chevrons.* The tower holds a set of bells that were recast in 1954 and rehung in the old oak frame installed in 1906. The original peal was of mixed age and quality. The oldest bell, the fifth, was cast in 1602 and the treble in 1906. Apart from the treble, they all appear to have been cast in the

West Country. The present peal is of excellent quality with the tenor bell weighing 10.5 cwt (508kg).

On the inside of St Mary's, the *arcade* is of a smaller type of late *Perpendicular* work with clustered *pillars* and wreathed *capitals,* frequently found in West Somerset. It has *four bays* which are wide and depressed, the *pillars* low, making it suitable for a church in such an exposed position. The research by historians on early wills indicate that the south *aisle* must have been built after 1532. George Elsworthy, the Rector who died in 1534 left the residue of his estate towards the building of the south *aisle* conditionally upon the work being finished within ten years. So historians know that the *pillars* and the arches and their carved *capitals* with the south *aisle* date between 1532-1542. A *Perpendicular font* stands just inside the door on the left-hand side. The basin is octagonal in shape with *quatrefoils* with leaves etc and supported by a stem with panels containing *ogee-arches addorsed* and *affronted.* Also on the west side is the *tower arch* with its continuous *chamfer.*

The *rood screen* in St Mary is one of the most exquisite pieces of work to be found in this part of the country. It consists of *four-light* sections in which each arch is subdivided into *two-light* arches and is *ribbed* and has panelling *coving.* It has four richly carved foliage *friezes* in the *cornice. The* lovely piece of ancient craftwork is one of the several generous gifts the church has been the recipient of in recent years. Originally it stood in the old church of St Audries near Watchet and is over 500 years old dating from the fifteenth century. When St Audries was rebuilt this screen was thrown out and stored in pieces in a barn. When it was discovered early in the present century efforts were made to find a suitable church in which to re-erect it. Exford church had the necessary proportions and size, and in 1929 the Bishop of Bath and Wells dedicated the re-erected screen. The restoration was very skilfully carried out by craftsmen of the London museums. Quite a large amount of the ancient carving has been preserved. The floor on the top of the *rood screen* is about four feet or more wide and was probably approached, in the screen's original home of St Audries, by a narrow flight of stairs cut in the thickness of the church wall. The screen is characteristic of the West England type being probably made in Dunster. Behind the *rood screen* is the east window which is *ogee-*

light arched and has a *tracery* which is of a delicate design and largely original. The *tracery* of the two windows on the north side of the *nave* are almost wholly original and of a similar design to those at Porlock and Winsford.

The *choir stalls* came from Queen's College, Cambridge. They have heavy tops made from a solid oak beam 14 feet wide and four inches thick similar to those used by monks but without the *Misericord* seats. The kneelers and cushions in the *sanctuary* at the communion rail and in the pews were all embroidered by the ladies of the Parish. The west *vestry* screen, erected in 1923 in memory of Hamilton Alexander Kingbike, is a splendid specimen of modern craftwork as it was given to the church in 1929 by Mr and Mrs Aston, local well-wishers, to mark their Golden Wedding anniversary. The organ is of a very mellow sound designed for a gentleman's voice and was presented to Exford church in 1924.

In the churchyard, the base of a cross and the shaft are all that is left of a cross that was probably standing here from before the Norman Conquest and may well be 500-900 years old. It is believed that the cross was knocked off by Oliver Cromwell's men. The view from the recently added porch (to protect the old door) is across the Exe Valley to the hills along the crest of which runs a prehistoric trackway used later for the cartage of tin etc from the West country mines to the Roman Portus Dubris (Dover) and Portus Lemenis (Lyme).

Methodist Church, Exford

Methodist Church, Exford

Although the Methodist church in Exford no longer exists, as with the one in Withypool, the building still remains. It was known to possess two stained glass windows by Burne-Jones which were unveiled in 1949. There is evidence in the building which suggests that it was used as a church in that the windows still have *round-headed* arches, quite frequently found in Methodist halls.

Again, like the hall in Withypool, in the past it has been converted into a dining area for an adjoining guest house - the Exmoor Guest House.

Church of St Mary the Virgin, Luccombe

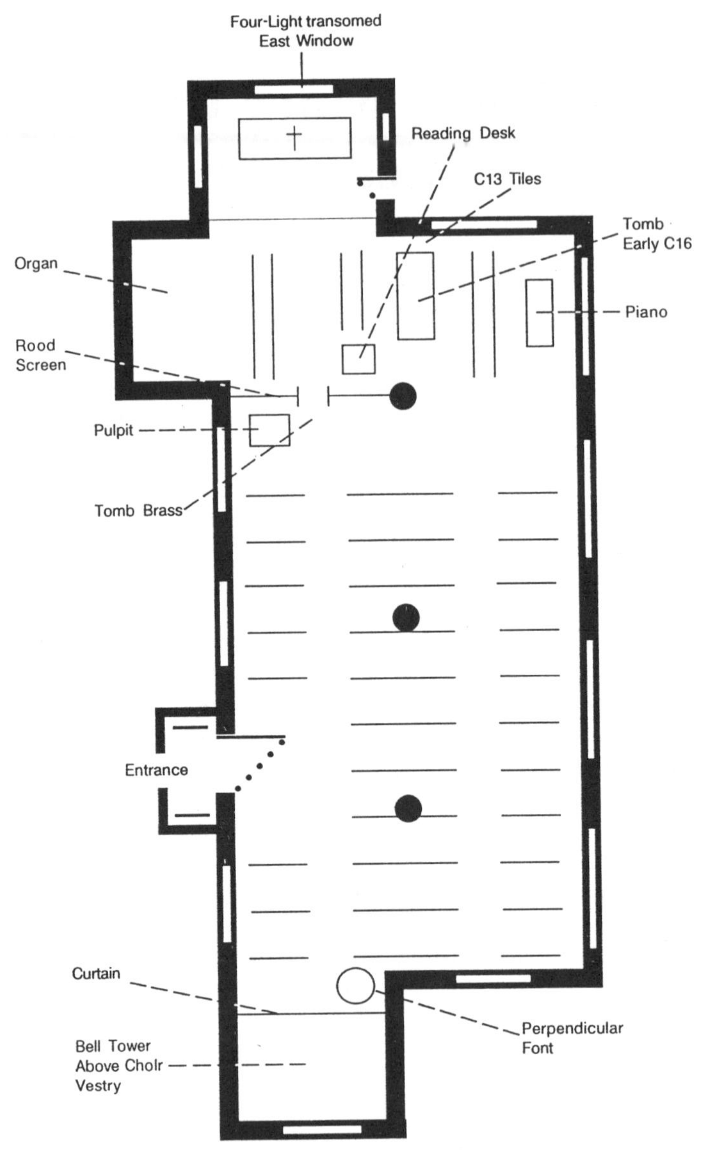

Plan of Church of St Mary the Virgin, Luccombe

Church of St Mary the Virgin, Luccombe

The church, on the edge of Exmoor, has its architectural roots in the *Early English* period (thirteenth century) and the fifteenth century. The impressive tall *three stage* tower is of the *Perpendicular* type of structure, supported by *diagonal buttresses* with *embattlements* and a higher square *stair turret*. This tower holds a set of six bells.

The only entry to the church is through a porch which protects the original door. Above this door there is a niche which once held a statue of the Virgin. There is a holy-water *stoup* in the west corner of the porch; the only signs of this now is a scoop in the wall. Towards the east is the moulded *tower arch* that leads eastwards into the thirteenth century *nave*. On the right-hand side of the tower arch, looking east, is an octagonal *Perpendicular font* with a panelled stem and pointed *quartrefoils* on the bowl. Eastwards is the *chancel*. In *front* of the low *rood screen* is a *tomb brass* which is of a particularly fine quality. The style of hair and the fashion of dress, Elizabethan ruff, can be very clearly seen. The tomb brass is in memory of William Harrison, who lived in Luccombe in the Manor House called 'Wychanger' (which is still standing today). The inscription at the bottom reads:

> "Here lies William Harrison, Gent who died and fell asleep on 18th day of the month of December, in the year of our Lord, 1615, years of age 76"

On the left of the *tomb brass* is a fine example of *Jacobean* work in the shape of the *pulpit*. This dates from the time between James I and Charles II (1660-1685). On the right of the tomb brass, between the *chancel* and the south *aisle*, stands a tomb which once stood under the tower. It has a flat top with two tiers of square panels decorated with big leaves. On the east side of this tomb, on the floor, are some thirteenth century tiles. They were found when the north porch was renovated and depict three *chevronels* of the Clare family, three lions of the Royal Arms and the figures of a bishop with a pastoral staff in his hand.

The south *aisle* was constructed in the fifteenth century. It consists of an *arcade* of *four-bays* supported by *piers* of *four-waves standard*. These *piers* replaced the original south wall. The *capitals* of these *piers* are decorated with finely carved bands of foliage. Halfway along this wall is a blocked-up doorway now housing some shelves upon which stand some early pieces of the thirteenth century church, and another holy-water *stoup*, similar to the one in the porch. The east window of the south *aisle* contains some old fragments of stained glass. Stained glass pale flowers in the south windows are similar to those in St Dubricius Church, Porlock as is the *tracery* of this window, with *four-lights* and a *transom*. The ceiling of the *aisle* continues into the thirteenth century roof of the *nave* making the roof one piece. This is known as a *coved* ceiling which is common in Devonshire and its bordering counties. It has carved *wall plates*, beams and *purlins* with very big *bosses*.

The *rood screen*, separating the *chancel* from the *nave*, incorporates bits to *tracery* and parts of the old *frieze*. On the right of the *sanctuary*, which is east of the *chancel*, is a niche containing a double *piscina* which led to a ground drain outside. Nearby is a seat or *sedile* for the priest. These two details are amongst the oldest thing in this church. On the *altar* stands a *cover* of 1816 and a *chalice* and two *patens* of 1843.

Some interesting monuments held by the church include one which is in memory of Dr Henry Byam, Rector in 1642, who served King Charles II and his ill-fated father.

In the churchyard, the stump of a fifteenth century cross stands. It is similar to one which stands in the churchyard of All Saints, Wootton Courtney. Both received the same kind of treatment which has been described as 'wanton vandalism' during its time! The poets Wordsworth and Coleridge were said to be inspired by the stump of an evergreen in the churchyard when they came to this parish.

All Saints Church, Wootton Courtenay

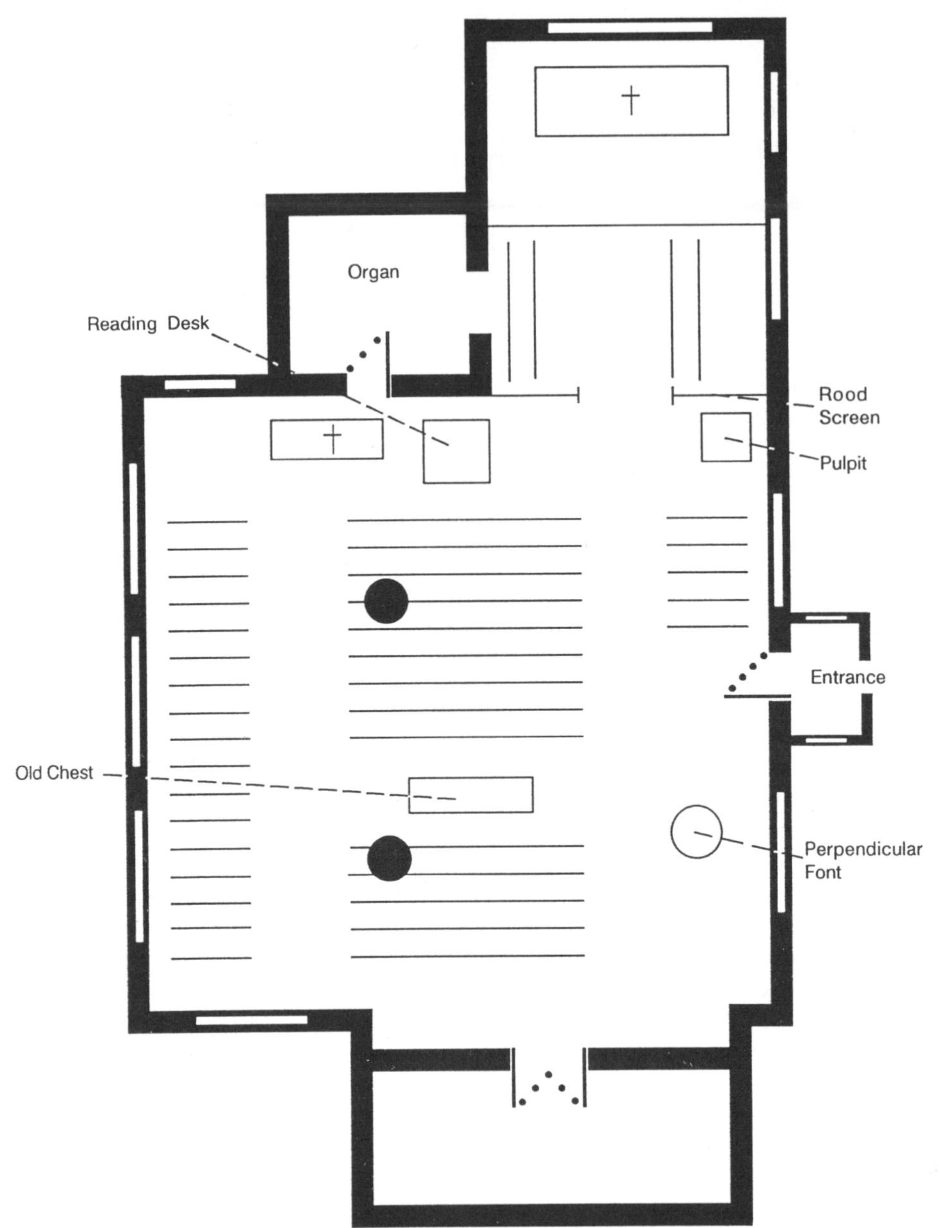

Plan of All Saints Church, Wootton Courtenay

All Saints Church, Wootton Courtenay

All Saints Church, Wootton Courtenay, is an ancient *Gothic* church with a *saddleback* tower and a beautifully carved roof. The oldest part of the existing church, the east end of the *chancel* and the lower part of the tower, date from about 1250, and may have formed part of a Norman church. The original tower was probably somewhat similar to the existing 1866 *saddleback* tower, but with a ridge running parallel to the church itself. The tower houses six bells dating from 1629 to 1903, the heaviest weighing 13 cwt (660 kg).

Unlike the Church of St Mary the Virgin, Luccombe, it has an unmoulded *tower arch* leading to the *nave*. Near the nineteenth century porch stands the octagonal *font* in the *Perpendicular* style, with a *quatrefoil frieze*. The porch, itself, contains an unusual holy-water *stoup*, unusual in that it was hewn from a single block of stone. There are carved figures of angels and animals inside and outside the porch. Except for the above mentioned, the rest of the church is of the fifteenth century. The north *arcade* and *aisle* were added in the mid-fifteenth century with its fine example of *wagon roofing*. The *aisle* has *four-waves standard* moulded *piers* with small round *capitals* only on the *shafts*. Both piers have big canopied statue niches (unusual place) facing towards the *nave*. At the base of the west *pier* stands a very old wooden chest similar to the one in Selworthy church. It, too, needed the presence of three people to open it as the three keys for the three cast iron bands were given to three people. The ceiling of the *aisle* has, like Luccombe, very large *bosses* carved with symbols depicting Evangelists eg a pelican, St George and the Dragon, the eagle of St John etc. New windows were provided by the *atelier* for the south side of the *nave* and the east window of the *aisle*, in 1530. These are similar to those at Selworthy and Luccombe.

The thirteenth century *chancel* has three stepped east *lancets* recently restored but, to certain people, seem over-restored. The *rood screen* is ornately carved in wood. When this screen was fitted in 1905, along with the building of the organ chamber and the *vestry,* a squint and an old entrance to a previous screen were discovered. Eastwards to the altar, stands the *chalice* and *cover* of 1573, *flagon* of 1624 and the *paten* presented in 1676, on the table under the east window. In the churchyard, the base block and part of the *shaft* of a sixteenth century cross, similar to that at Luccombe, are situated near a great Yew tree which is alleged to date back to the time of the Black Death of 1350.

Appendices

Appendix A1

The Methodist Church, Bossington

Appendix A1 contd ...

The Methodist Church, Porlock Weir

Appendix A1 contd ...

The Methodist Church, Porlock

The above three churches were initially included in the main part of the project. As the churches were closed to the public, enough information could not be gathered.

Appendix A2

St Michael's Church, Minehead

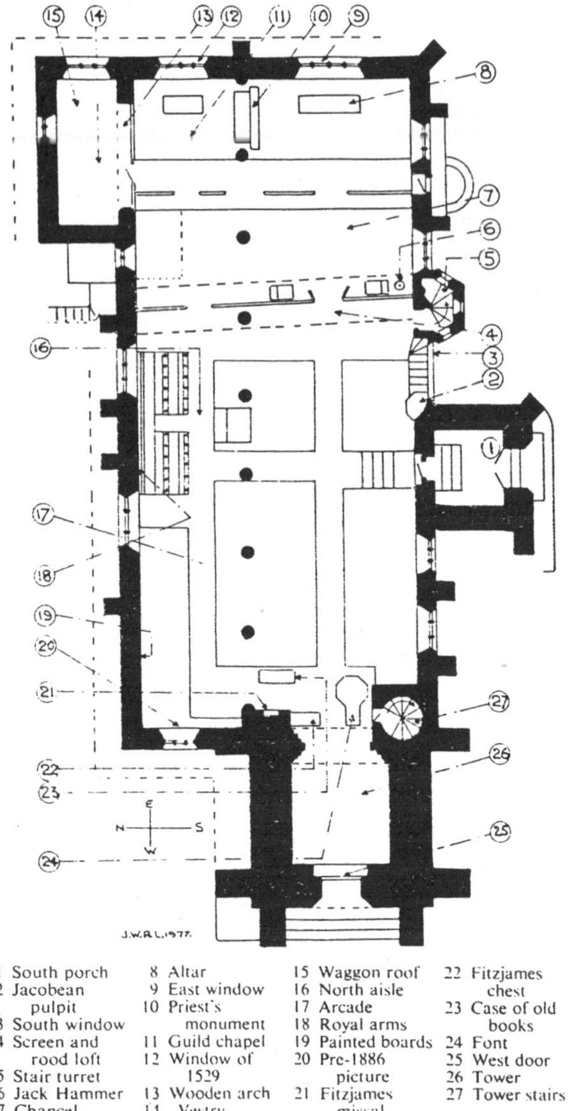

Plan of St Michael's Church, Minehead

St Michael's Church, Minehead

St Michael is a dedication usually for churches on rocks or hills. The Minehead church lies against the side of a steep hill, North Hill. It is a large church made of light grey stone with a big west tower with set-back *buttresses*, *battlements*, little square *pinnacles* and a higher south east *stair turret*. On the west side of the tower is a window with *four-lights* and a *transom*. Above this and on two other sides there are bell-openings with one *transom*. On the south side there is a niche with the representation of the Trinity, God holding Christ crucified whilst on the east side there is a relief with an unusual combination of St Michael and the Virgin of the Misericord (sheltering little human beings under her mantle).

The church consists of a *nave, embattled* on the south side with *quatrefoils* in the *battlements*, a south porch, *rood turret* and an *unembattled chancel*. Inside, by the way of windows, there is a large *four-light* window at the east end of the *chancel*, otherwise the other windows in the rest of the church are *two-light* with or without a *transom*. The north *arcade* consists of eight bays ie there is no division between the *nave* and the *chancel*. The *arcade* is supported by slim octagonal *piers* capped by fifteenth century *capitals* and interwoven with *double-chamfered* arches. At the west end of the *nave*, a moulded tower arch from the fifteenth century separates the *nave* from the base of the tower. At the east end of the nave is an arch that leads into the *vestry*, formerly a *chantry chapel* which is made from oak and is broad and rustic. The roof of the *vestry*, like that of the *nave* and *chancel*, is of the *wagon*-type.

In a church of this size and age many furnishings and treasures are kept. For example, the *font*, under the tower arch, is octagonal and of the *perpendicular* period of construction. It has a richly panelled stem and seated, on the ledge at the foot of the bowl, are figures, their legs hanging over the underside.

Separating the *nave* and the *aisle* from the *chancel*, is the *rood screen* which has a *dado* with similar *quartrefoils* left and right of the *ogee arches* to those on the windows in the *nave*. It is *ribbed* and has panelled *coving* and sharply carved *foliage friezes* between the *four-light* sections, the arches being subdivided into two of *two lights*. Also in the *nave* is a mid-seventeenth century *pulpit* with *Jacobean friezes* but no longer, with its panels. On top of the *aisle* screen stands a clock-jack, Jack Hammer, ie a rustically painted eighteenth century figure of a man formerly with a hammer to strike the hours.

The *chancel chapels* come forward as far as the *chancel* to form a group of three windows under three *gables*. On the *altar* is a *chalice* of 1624, a 1674 *paten*, a *flagon* of 1705 and another *chalice* and *paten* presented in 1731. A chandelier made of brass and dated 1727 hangs high above the *altar*.

Around the church are other monuments such as a *tomb brass* to a Lady of a high status in the society, probably laid about 1440, measuring 28 inches in length. There is also a *tomb chest* with eight empty niches.

Appendix A3

St Peter's Chapel, Minehead

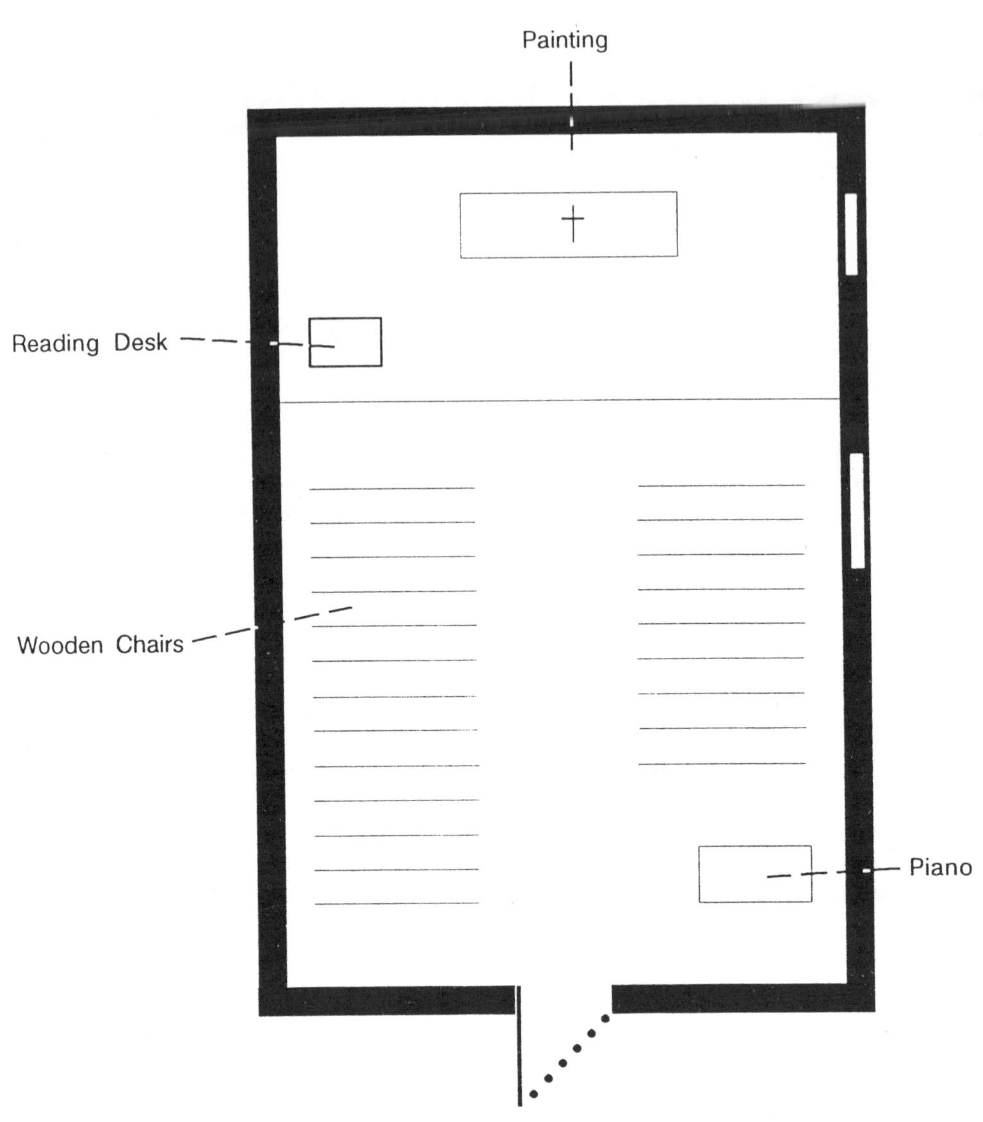

Plan of St Peter's Chapel, Minehead

St Peter's Chapel, Minehead

This building is all that is left of one that was erected about 1628 as a storehouse, by Robert Quirke, a shipowner and merchant of Minehead. After his death it was to be rented out to provide an income to endow Quirke's *Almshouses*, which are still to be seen in Market House Lane in Minehead.

The present building is the outer of two cellars, the inner having been pulled down when the Pier Hotel was built, about 1899. Around 1830, the property was taken over by the Parish but by 1887 it had fallen into disrepair. Later the upper storey became a seaman's shelter and in the early 1900's (about 1910) the Rev F M Etherington, the Vicar of Minehead, converted the ground floor into a *chapel* for the people of Quay Town.

The *almshouses* connected with this property were built in 1630 and over the door of one house is a plate recording the bequest. Tradition has it that Quirke and his brother were caught in a great storm at sea and vowed that if saved, they would sell both ship and cargo, and give the money to the poor of Minehead. The ship's timbers were used in building the *almshouses* and the bell in the bell cote on the outside of the *chapel* is said to be the ship's bell.

Robert Quirke was a *burgess* in Queen Elizabeth I's reign. He was also, for a time, one of the churchwardens. There is a unique memorial to him in St Michael's church, Minehead, on the wall of the north *aisle* in the form of a seventeenth century *reredos*, consisting of a series of *round headed* panels on which are painted the Apostles' Creed, the Lord's Prayer and figures of Moses and Aaron. At the base of one of the panels is the inscription:

> "Robert Quirke the sonne of James Quirke gave this to the Church.
> Anno 1637"

The interior of St Peter's is very simple, being painted blue in colour and has plain wooden chairs for the worshippers to be seated on. The *reredos* behind the *altar* is of Jesus standing and watching over the sea on which the Emma Louise, Minehead's last coal ship, sailed (pictured above). On either side of the *altar* there are two white statues; on the right, one of Jesus, whilst on the left, one of a big bird.

Appendix A4

St Andrew's Church, Minehead

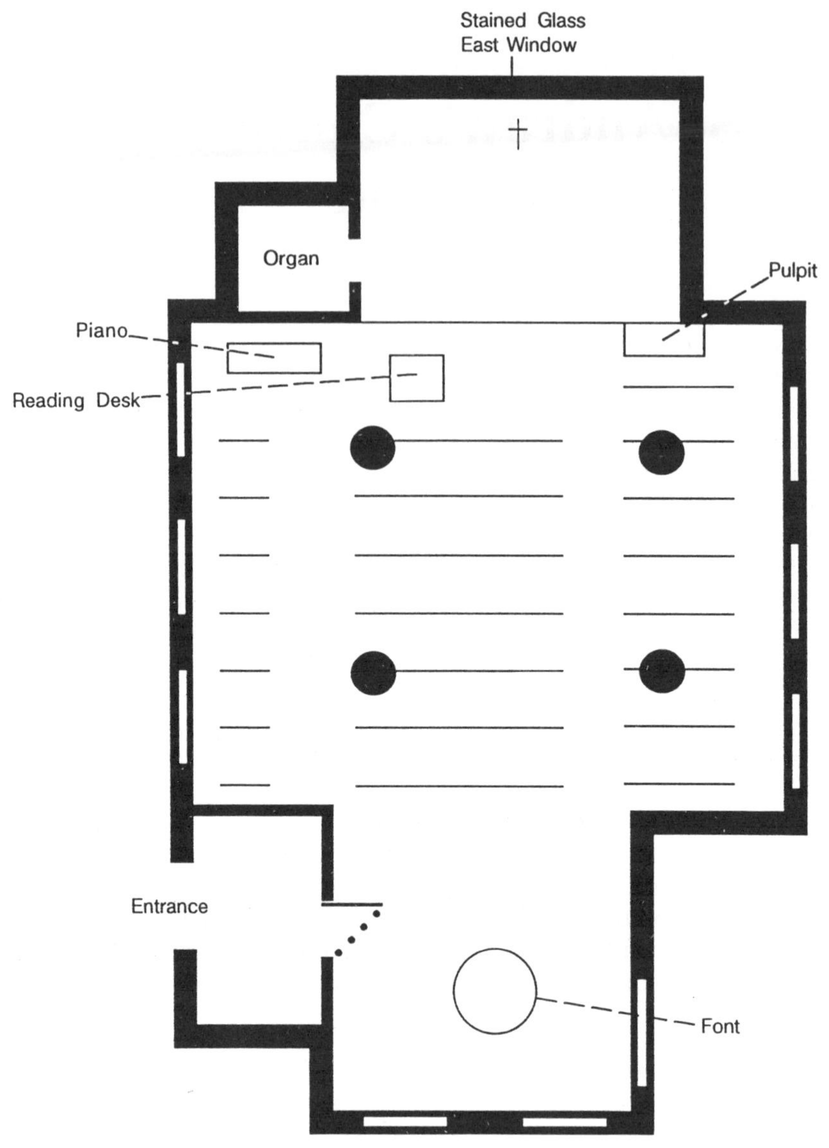

Plan of St Andrew's Church, Minehead

St Andrew's Church, Minehead

St Andrew's Church is situated off Wellington Square, in Minehead. It was built in 1880 by G E Street and made from red sandstone. A tower was planned to be built at the south west end of the church, which is unusual as they are traditionally built at the west end, but it never materialised. A *buttress* was built up the front of the west end. The roof is plain with *hammer-beams* and *arched braces*.

The interior of the church is very plain in comparison to Minehead's other large church, St Michael's. It has a *tracery* on the west window in the style of the thirteenth and the early fourteenth century. The *arcade piers* are octagonal without *capitals*, the arches dying into them. There are heavy *hood-moulds* on unmoulded *corbels*. The *nave* has a small *clerestory*. The *chancel arch* separating the *nave* from the *chancel* is marked by a plain wooded boarding. The stained glass in the east window was crafted in 1889 by Kempe.

In front of the church, off Wellington Square, stands a statue of Queen Anne under a Victorian canopy. It is, as experts say, an uncommonly fine piece of work with great skill in the rendering of the details of the clothes. It was made in 1719, out of alabaster, possibly by Francis Bird. It originally stood at the east end of the north *aisle* of St Michael's church.

Glossary

addorsed
two human figures, animals, or birds, etc placed symmetrically so that they turn their backs to each other.

affronted
two human figures, animals, or birds, etc placed symmetrically so that they face each other.

aisle
part of a church parallel to the nave and choir, and separated from them by pillars; passage between rows of seats or pews.

almsdish
silver, gold or brass plate used to collect money for the poor.

almshouse
house endowed by a private charity where poor can be received.

altar
raised structure with a flat top, on which Holy Communion is offered.

altar crucifix
the crucifix which stands on the altar.

anchorite
religious recluse, hermit.

arcade
range of arches supported on piers or columns, or free-standing.

arched braces
see brace.

atelier
artist's studio (French).

baluster
small pillar or column of fanciful outline.

barrel-beamed roof
timber roof.

battlement
parapet with a series of indentations or embrasures with raised portions.

bay
internal compartments of a building; each divided from the other not by solid walls but by divisions only marked in the side walls (Columns, pilasters, etc) or the ceiling (beams etc).

boss
knob or projection usually placed to cover the intersection of ribs in a vault.

box-pew
pew with a high wooden enclosure.

brace
inclined timbers inserted in a roof to strengthen other timbers can be straight or arched.

burgess
citizen, dweller in borough having full municipal right.

buttress
mass of brickwork or masonry projecting from a wall to give additional strength.

canopy
projection or hood over an altar, pulpit, niche, statue etc.

capital
head or top part of a column or pier.

chalice
cup used in the Communion service.

chamfer
surface made by cutting across the square angle of a stone block, piece of wood etc at an angle of 45° to the other two surfaces.

chancel
that part of the east end of a church in which the altar is placed, usually applied to the whole continuation of the nave east of the crossing.

chancel arch
arch at the west end of the chancel.

chantry chapel
chapel attached to, or inside, a church, endowed for the saying of Masses for the soul of the founder or some other individual.

chapel
place of worship having no parish attached to it, place set aside for worship in a nobleman's house.

chevrons
sculptured moulding forming a zigzag.

chevronel
smaller versions of chevron.

choir stall
pews in the sanctuary where the choir is seated.

clerestory
the upper part of the nave, choir and trancepts, containing a series of windows.

clock-jack
stone figure that holds a hammer to strike a bell.

corbel
block of stone projecting from a wall, supporting some horizontal feature.

cornice
in classical architecture the top section of the entablature. Also for a projecting decorative feature along the top of a wall, arch etc.

cover
cover to a Communion cup.

coving
concave undersurface in the nature of a hollow moulding but on a larger scale.

cusp
projecting point between the foils in a foiled Gothic arch.

dado
decorative covering of the lower part of a wall.

diagonal buttress
one placed against the right angle formed by two walls, and more or less equiangular with both.

domestic-looking
windows that look like those of houses window etc.

Doric
oldest, strongest and the simplest of the three Greek order of architecture.

double-chamfered
two chamfered arches on window/arches.

Early English
historical division of Gothic architecture roughly covering the thirteenth century.

effigy
three-dimensional representation of a person.

embattlement
a parapet which has battlements.

entablature
in classical architecture the whole of the horizontal members above a column, ie the frieze, cornice etc.

flagon
vessel for the wine used in the Communion service.

fleuron
small flower-like ornament.

flying buttress
arch or half arch transmitting the trust of a vault or roof from the upper part of a wall to an outer support or buttress.

foil
lobe formed by the cusping of a circle or an arch. Trefoil, quartrefoil, cinquefoil, multifoil etc express the number of leaf shapes to be seen.

font
basin for baptismal water.

four bay
a bay with four internal compartments.

four-hollow section
usually applies to a pier with a square cross-section of concave sides.

four-hollow standard
pier with four hollow tubes of metal as section support.

four-light window
a window with four lights.

four-waves section
usually applies to a pier with a square cross-section of wavy sides.

four-waves standard
usually applies to a pier with a square cross-section of wavy sides.

frieze
middle division of a classical entablature.

gable
triangular piece of wall enclosed by ends of ridged roof; triangular decoration over window or door.

gargoyle
carved rain-water spout on roof.

Gothic
period of architecture from about 1150 to about 1530 pertaining to a medieval style of pointed arches.

hammer-beams
beam projecting at right angles usually from the top of a wall, to carry arched braces or struts and arched braces.

holy vessels
religious goblets, flagons etc.

hood-mould
projecting moulding above an arch or a lintel to throw off water.

imposts
brackets in walls usually formed of mouldings, on which the ends of an archrest.

Jacobean
period of architecture during the reign of James I.

jamb
straight side of an archway, doorway, or window.

label
square-arched projecting moulding on the arch over a door or a window, which extends horizontally across the opening and returns vertically downwards for a short distance.

lancet windows
lender pointed-arched window.

light
opening between the mullion of a window.

lintel
horizontal beam or stone bridging an opening.

Living
benefice held by a rector or vicar.

metope
in classical architecture of the Doric order, the space in the frieze between the triglyph.

misericord
bracket placed on the under side of a hinged choir stall seat which, when turned up, provided the occupant of the seat with a support during long periods of standing.

mullion
vertical post or upright dividing a window into two or more lights.

nave
central part of a church west of the chancel.

Non-Gothic
period of architecture other than the Gothic period.

ogee arch
Moghul type arch.

one-light
window with one light.

parvise
room over a church porch. Often used as a school-house or as a storeroom.

paten
plate to hold the bread at Communion or Mass.

pavillion
parvise with a gallery.

Perpendicular
historical division of English Gothic architecture roughly covering the period from 1350 to 1530.

pier
strong, solid support, frequently square in section. Also called a pillar.

pilaster
shallow pier attached to a wall.

pillar
stone column supporting a structure.

pinnacle
ornamental form crowning a spire, tower, buttress etc usually of steep pyramidal, conical, or some similar shape.

piscina
basin for washing the Communion or Mass vessels, provided with a drain. Generally set in or against the wall to the south of an altar.

Pre-reformation
period of architecture before 1450.

pulpit
raised enclosed platform from which a preacher delivers a sermon.

purlin
longitudinal member laid parallel with the wall plate and ridge beam some way up the slope of the roof.

quartrefoil
four-leafed foil.

rafter
one of a series of inclined structures to which a roof covering is fixed.

reading desk
tall stand from which Bible lesson are read.

relief
method of carving figures so as to project from a flat background surface.

reredos
structure behind and above the altar.

ribbing
wood work raised from background.

Romanesque
that style in architecture which was current in the eleventh and twelfth century and preceded the Gothic style. Also called the Norman style.

rood screen
screen at the west end of the chancel.

root turret
a turret built over a large crucifix which is usually set over the chancel entrance.

round headed
window or arch with a semicircular or window/arch curved top.

rubble
building stones, not square or hewn, nor laid in regular courses.

saddleback
tower roof shaped like an ordinary gabled.

Saltire Cross
equal-limbed cross placed diagonally.

sanctuary
area around the main altar of a church.

set-back buttress
angle buttress set slightly back from the angle.

segmental arch
arch with a segmented top.

sedile
recessed seat within the altar rails.

shaft
tall column. Also known as a pier.

spandrel
triangular surface between one side of an arch, the horizontal drawn from its apex, and the vertical drawn from its springer, also the surface between two arches.

spine/spire
tall pyramidal or conical pointed erection often built on top of a tower, turret etc.

square headed
window or arch with a flat top. window/arch.

squint
hole cut in a wall or through a pier to allow a view of the main altar of a church from places whence it could not otherwise be seen.

stair turret
very small tower, round or polygonal in plan and housing a small spiral staircase.

stoup
vessel for the reception of holy-water, usually placed near a door.

stilted window/arch
semi-circular top to an arch or window.

straight headed
similar to a square headed window/arch.

strut
upright timber connecting the tie-beam with the rafter above it.

terminal
upper part of human figure growing out of a pier, pilaster etc, which tapers towards the base.

three-light window
window with three lights.

three-stage tower
tower built at three different times.

tomb-brass
engraved brass plate in memory of an individual.

tomb-chest
chest-shaped stone coffin, the most usual medieval form of funeral monument.

tower arch
archway between the base of the tower and the nave.

tracery
intersecting ribwork in upper part of a window, or used decoratively in blank arches, on vaults etc.

transom
horizontal bar across the opening of a window.

triglyph
blocks with vertical grooves separating the metopes in the Doric frieze.

two-light
window with two lights (panes).

two-stage tower
tower built at two different times.

vault
arched roof.

vestry
part of a church where ceremonial garments worn by clergy, and records are kept.

wagon-roof
roof in which by closely set rafters with arched braces the appearance of the inside of the canvas tilt over a wagon is achieved. Wagon-roof can be panelled (ceiled) or left uncovered.

wall plate
timber laid longitudinally on the top of a wall.

Bibliography

AUTHOR(S)	TITLE (EDITION)	PUBLISHERS
Addison W Sir	Local Styles of the English Parish Church (1st Ed)	Batsford Ltd
Brabbs D	England Country Churches (1st Ed)	Weidenfeld & Nicolson
Burton S H	Exmoor (4th Ed)	Rewood Burn Ltd
Clowney P & C	Exploring Churches (1st Ed)	Lion
Garmonsway G N	The Penguin English Dictionary (1st Ed)	Penguin Books Ltd
Lowther K & Hammond R	North Devon and Exmoor (1st Ed)	Ward Lock Ltd
Pevsner N	The Buildings of England South and West Somerset (1st Ed)	Penguin Books Ltd

More information was gathered from leaflets provided in the churches, historical notes displayed and from discussions with local people.

My Thanks To ...

My sincere thanks to the 2nd Selsdon and Addington Scout Group for letting me join their annual summer camp held last year (1986) and this year (1987) at Horner, near Porlock, Somerset; to some of the boys, who accompanied me on some of the hikes; to their Group leader Tom Buckett* and his wife, Paddy; to a former leader, Tom Allan and his wife, Dot, who now reside in Porlock; to Ted Cook, who often joined me on the walks, and his wife Mary; to Graeme Bridger, who took me to some distant churches, and his wife Pam; to Karen Holden, who accompanied me on a tour of churches and to Richard Waple for his help in transporting me to some of them.

Also thanks to my father for some basic instructions on draftsmanship and to my mother for assisting me with architectural terminology. Last, but not least, thanks to my brother, Shailesh, for dealing with my word processor problems and putting up with my endless typing. I had taken over his room, although initially it was just the computer desk, but by the time I finished the project, my papers were all over his working desk, floor, chairs and on his bed, thus forcing him out of his room temporarily!

Finally, my very sincere thanks to the DOE Award Scheme and its organisers for providing me with the opportunity during the past five years to learn a variety of new skills and to explore in some detail the environment we live in. Without the DOE Award Scheme it would not have been possible for me to appreciate some of the skills essential not only for the development of individuals like me but to recognise the need to use them to serve the community whenever possible. For example, Red Cross First Aid, Home Nursing, Gingerbread Children's Playgroup and the Conservation of National Trust properties are some of the activities I was involved in when preparing for the Bronze, Silver and Gold Awards.

* In 1990, Tom Buckett received a BEM for community service.

Footnote: I would like to thank Mr. Bill Walker and other members of staff at the Youth Office, Taberner House, Croydon Council.

DoE Award Section

Extracts from the Author's DoE Record Book Related to Gold Award Activities

GOLD AWARD
Residential Project

Event National Trust Acorn Camp.

Purpose Conserving habitats.

Place Henman Basecamp, Surrey.

Dates of attendance 3·7·86 - 10·7·86

Assessor's report (including personal standards, relationships with others, responsibility, initiative, and general progress)

Sharmila worked well throughout the week, showing interest & enthusiasm at what could be a difficult task. She participated well within the group, and was a definite asset to it.

Signed Virginia Cooke Date 10·7·86

Qualification Acorn Camp leader.

38

Service

Form of service

COMMUNITY SERVICE

Training organised by GINGERHEAD PLAYSCHOOL

Dates 21-1-85 TO 3-3-86

Training completed or qualification gained (as appropriate)

Assessor's report:

Form of practical service undertaken

Dates

Assessor's report: SHARMILA IS A VERY HIGH QUALITY VOLUNTEER. SHE IS CHEERFUL, CAPABLE AND WILL TURN HER HAND TO ANY TASK. SHE HAS BEEN MOST HELPFUL IN THE CRAFTS AND IS WELL LIKED BY ALL.

Where practical service has been given, it is certified that three counselling sessions were held.

Signed [illegible] Date 3-3-86

Qualification PLAYLEADER

39

GOLD AWARD
Practical Service

This page is intended for use when more than one form of practical service is undertaken during the twelve month period.

Form(s) of practical service undertaken

Dates

Assessor's report:

It is certified that three counselling sessions were held.

Signed ______________ Date ______________

Qualification ______________

Expeditions

Preliminary Training

Subject	Instructor's signature	Date
Safety Precautions		
Casualty Code		
Map Reading	J a Buckett	23/30-8-86
Use of Compass	J a Buckett	23/30-8-86
Food and Cooking	J a Buckett	23/30-8-86
Country Code	J a Buckett	23/30-8-86
Observations and Recording		
Further training as appropriate		
Purpose work		
Campcraft or Hostelling	J a Buckett.	23/30-8-86
Proficiency in chosen form of travel	J a Buckett	23/30-8-86
Transport and Timetables		
Highway Code		

It is certified that a satisfactory standard of training has been reached in the subjects indicated above, that one/~~two/three~~* practice journeys have been completed and that this participant is properly equipped for the qualifying venture. For ventures in wild country (see inside back cover) the expedition panel for the area has been notified.

* delete as appropriate

Signed J a Buckett. AGSL. Date 2/10/86

GOLD AWARD
Expeditions—Qualifying Venture

Nature of ~~Expedition~~/Exploration/~~Adventurous~~ Project On foot and Camping for three nights

Area EXMOOR

Dates 30-8-87 — 4-9-87

Purpose Survey of Churches on Exmoor

Assessor's report

of venture: TO EXPLORE THE MOORLANDS, THE EXMOOR VILLAGES AND THE VILLAGE CHURCH. COVERING AN AREA OF 25 TO 30 MILES. EACH COURSE BEING PLOTTED ON AN OS MAP USING COMPASS BEARINGS

of participant's oral or written account: HAS THE ABILITY TO FAMILIARISE VERY QUICKLY WITH THE AREA AND ALSO SHOWS A GOOD WORKING KNOWLEDGE OF COMPASS & MAP.

Signed [signature] Date 4-9-87

Qualification A.D.C SCOUT WEST SOMERSET.

This page may be used if space on page 42 is insufficient.

Sharmila's 75 page report 'Churches on Exmoor' has been produced with great care and attention to detail. Descriptions of each church are accompanied by a photograph and a plan. Preface, Brief description of Exmoor, Map, Appendices, Glossary and Bibliography complete a thoroughly well-researched and expert treatment of the subject.

I ~~would~~ judge Sharmila's report to be a model of its kind and it stands as a tribute to the excellence of the Duke of Edinburgh's Award Scheme.

Signed David Watson Date 11/2/88

Rector, St John the Divine Church Selsdon

GOLD AWARD
Skills

Skill(s) followed Indoor Rifle Shooting.

Date started 09.04.84 completed 26.02.86.

Assessor's report:

Sharmila has taken to Indoor Shooting very well indeed. She is a determined young lady and has the temperament needed for this skill. Her concentration is good and consistently shoots well.

It has been a pleasure to teach her to this standard, though much of the work has been made

It is certified that this participant also has an understanding of the practical, cultural and social aspects of the chosen activity or topic.

Signed [signature] Capt Date 26.02.86.

Qualification Weapon Training Instructor

This page may be used if a second skill is followed or if space on page 44 is insufficient.

easier through her enthusiastic approach to the subject.

GOLD AWARD
Physical Recreation
Points required: 36

Participation			**Points**
Activity CRICKET			
Date started 16·2·85 completed 16·4·86			
Number of sessions 18 (A)			36
Signature of coach or instructor [signature]			
Standards attained			
Activity chosen	Event(s)	Standard(s)	
	Total for standards (B)		
	Total points (A) + (B)		36

Improvement. It is certified that this participant has shown improvement in application, technique, skill, tactics, fitness, knowledge of rules, appreciation of hazards and knowledge of safety precautions, as appropriate to the activity chosen.

Signature of assessor [signature]

Qualification Teacher Date 17·4·1986

Certificates and Awards

This is to certify that:

SHARMILA PRABHU.

has satisfactorily observed the conditions and met the requirements in each section of the Scheme, and is now qualified for the following Award.

BRONZE AWARD

Signed W.M. Walker

Appointment ASSISTANT YOUTH SERVICE ADVISER.

Operating Authority LONDON BOROUGH OF CROYDON

Date JAN 12TH 1984.

SILVER AWARD

Signed W.M. Walker

Appointment AWARDS OFFICER. A.Y.S.A.

Operating Authority LONDON BOROUGH OF CROYDON

Date 12TH AUG. 1985.

GOLD AWARD

Signed [signature]

Appointment DIRECTOR OF EDUCATION.

Operating Authority LONDON BOROUGH OF CROYDON

Date 21-3-1988.

Reproduced with kind permission from the Croydon Advertiser July 29, 1988

Gold award launches new project

A FORMER pupil of Croydon High School received her Duke of Edinburgh's Gold Award from the Mayor of Croydon, Coun Derek Loughborough, at Fairfield Halls on Friday.

Sharmila Prabhu, is now a student at Kent University.

She received her award after several years' work covering a wide range of activities, ranging from helping young children to an archaeology survey, from country dancing to compiling a book on churches in the West Country.

Sharmila described her many activities to gain the award at a lunch and meeting to set up Croydon's Duke of Edinburgh's Award Scheme Industrial Project.

The objective is to form a committee of business people in the town to promote and develop a scheme to enable young people to continue in the award scheme when they start work.

At present some who start the award scheme at school or college have difficulty in continuing with it later.

The project aims to find meeting places and training facilities, obtain funding, and recruit part-time voluntary staff to assist those working for the award.

A committee to set up the industrial project will be established following the meeting.

Mayor's Parlour
Town Hall
Katharine Street
Croydon CR9 1XW

Sharmila Prabhu has provided an example of the high levels of achievement possible by participants in the Duke of Edinburgh Award Scheme. Once she obtained her Gold Medal she did not let her involvement with the Scheme lapse. She helped launch the Croydon Duke of Edinburgh Commercial Project, established to offer opportunities to young people in their workplace, thus broadening the scope of the Scheme locally.

Croydon is very proud of its Scheme, and rightly so, as it allows many young people through schools, youth organisations and commerce and industry, to progress through the various stages, to tackle the many challenges, physical, intellectual and emotional, and through the process to make the transition from childhood to responsible adulthood.

Young people are the citizens of tomorrow. The Scheme provides evidence, if evidence be needed, that our future is secure. Sharmila provides an example of what young people can achieve if given both the opportunity and the support from adults in the local community.

I am delighted to commend her book to you and wish her good luck and success for the future.

Jim Walker

Mayor

(Councillor Jim Walker - Mayor)

On the gold run

CRICKET player Sharmila Prabhu was bowled over after receiving her gold Duke of Edinburgh award.

Sharmila, 21, was presented with the gold award by Prince Philip at St James' Palace, last week.

She chose cricket as the physical recreation activity of the award. She still plays for Wallington Ladies Cricket Club. In 1984, she played for the under-19s Surrey ladies team.

An ex-Croydon High School pupil, Sharmila now has a degree in accountancy and computing, and has a summer job with Nestle in the data processing department.

To gain the award, which she finished in 1988, she played cricket, practised rifle shooting, helped with the Gingerbread play group a couple of times a week, did a week's conservation work with a National Trust acorn camp and undertook an expedition on Exmoor.

A project on Exmoor churches may be printed in booklet form as a model for future participants.

One church, at Oare, is where R D Blackmore's heroine, Lorna Doone, dies on the altar.

"Doing the award brings out qualities other than scholastic, and you get the back up and support to do things you otherwise wouldn't have the chance to do," she said.

Sharmila was awarded the Queen's Guide Award in 1985.

[Photo: Dave Smith No: 892590

The Author's DoE Activities

Sharmila was born in 1968 in Croydon, Surrey. Through her involvement in the Girl Guide movement, she obtained the Queen's Guide Award in 1984 from the 2nd Selsdon & Addington Guide Unit. Her project for the Queen's Guide Award on India was based on her visit there including a trip to the Taj Mahal. It was highly commended by the Guide District Commissioner and her Unit Leaders for the standard it achieved.

When she was 10 years old, she won an industrial scholarship to attend Croydon High School, an independent school in Selsdon. At the age of 14, she joined the Duke of Edinburgh (DoE) Scheme run by the school and completed the Bronze Award in 1983, Silver in 1985 and Gold just before her 19th birthday.

According to her speech at the launch of the Croydon Commercial Project, it was not a smooth ride to the Gold Award. In extremely cold and wet conditions during a March weekend when BST started, she failed in her Expedition Section for the Silver Award. Carrying heavy and wet camping equipment on her back and walking on country roads to the required destination in severe weather conditions, her legs failed her to the extent that she just could not continue with only a few miles separating her from what would have been an eventful but successful expedition. She asked the other three girls in her group to continue in the hope that they would complete the required walk.

Sharmila, however, had to be rescued by the teacher waiting at the reporting station. Her idea, of staying behind on her own, backfired because her group failed on the grounds that the group as a whole did not complete the walk.

It was decision time and she decided that she did not want to continue with the Scheme. But time was a great healer and with parental persuasion over a period of time, she changed her mind and continued with the Scheme. Mistakes are to be learnt from, never forgotten. Since then, she has never looked back.

As part of DoE activities, she gained the British Red Cross First Aid and Home Nursing adult certificates, and represented the school in Junior and Senior cricket teams. She was awarded the School Cricket Progress cup and represented the Surrey U19 ladies cricket team.

Her other DoE activities included an archaeological survey, country dancing and indoor rifle shooting. Captain Reddy, Weapons Training Officer at a local Combined Cadet Forces centre, said in the assessor's report: "She has the temperament needed for this skill. Her concentration is good and she consistently shoots well ... A pass mark of 94% reflects the effort given to this demanding skill. A pleasant and cheerful young lady throughout the period."

Rector of St John the Divine Church of Selsdon, Rev L A D Watson, said in his assessment of Sharmila's project on Exmoor Churches for the Gold Award: "I would judge Sharmila's report to be a model of its kind and it stands as a tribute to the excellence of the Duke of Edinburgh Award Scheme."

The leader of the Gingerbread playgroup, where Sharmila completed her service, said in his assessment: "Sharmila is a very high quality volunteer. She is cheerful, capable and will turn her hand to any task. She has been most helpful in the crafts and is well liked by all."

Miss Goddard, the mathematics and computer training teacher at Croydon High School, said in her assessment in 1983 of her computing skills at the Bronze Award level: "Sharmila has written two good programs; the first was a language program for French or German involving graphics. The second program was a game of guessing the number. Through her reading, she has acquired a knowledge of the history of computers." In the same year, Lt Whyt, RNR ATO, said in his assessment report of the expedition for the Bronze Award: "A well planned expedition which showed a good grasp of map and camp craft skills. Sharmila participated in a well written account of the group's investigation and expedition."

After her speech, as a Gold Award recipient, from the Croydon Mayor's table at the launch of the scheme's industrial project at Fairfield Halls, Mr David Morrison, Chairman of the London Borough of Croydon Co-ordinating Committee for the DoE Award Scheme said in his letter to Sharmila: "... I am sure it did more than the contributions of the professionals in giving the Mayor's guests an insight into what can be achieved through the scheme."

Miss Mark, Headmistress at Croydon High School, said in her annual report speech in January 1989: "It was a pleasure to hear Sharmila Prabhu, now at the University of Kent studying accountancy, introduce the Gold Civic Presentation in the Arnhem Gallery with much confidence and assurance, and to learn that she had been involved during the summer in Croydon's bid to interest industry and business in providing support for the scheme for the young employed".

The text of this book was written in 1987 as the DoE Gold Award project report and since then she has received the Gold Award in a ceremony at St James' Palace in the presence of HRH Prince Philip. She is a keen supporter of the Scheme because she feels that it had offered her the opportunity during the five years she was actively involved in gaining the awards, to learn a variety of new skills and to explore in some detail the environment we live in.

In April 1990, she represented the DoE Scheme in the launch of Prince Charles' Volunteers at St James' Palace. There were over 350 guests, mostly senior executives from many sectors of industry, and included HRH Prince Charles, the Home Secretary and the Speaker of the House of Commons. Sharmila spoke about her volunteer work within the scheme.

The Times (April 25, 1990), on the day of the launch, reported the story with a headline "Prince launches his cheristed Charlie's Angels". Alan

Hamilton, the reporter, said in the opening paragraph: "The Prince of Wales will today launch his long-cherished national schemo for community service which is to be known officially as The Volunteers but is more likely to enter the popular consciousness as Charlie's Angels."

Mr Bernard Weatherill MP, the Speaker of the House of Commons, said in his letter to Sharmila: "... My purpose in writing to you is to congratulate you most warmly on the confident way in which you spoke at the launch ... You provided an admirable example of what participating in the volunteer programme is designed to achieve." Mr David Parker, the organiser of the launch, said in his letter to Sharmila: "... to say a big personal thank you for the tremendous contributions you have made to the launch of Volunteers on April 25 ... Your speech was very welcome indeed. His Royal Highness was delighted with what you said and the way you put your message across so professionally ..."

Sharmila is now a graduate with honours in Accounting with Computing from the University of Kent. She is presently pursuing a career in accountancy.

Bernard Doswell JP, BA, MSc.
Youth Service Adviser
London Borough of Croydon